Semper Fi

KOREA

THE LAST OF THE FUN WARS

From the Beach to the Reservoir
& Other Heroic Events

KAL & ANETTE KALNASY

Copyright © 2001 Kal Kalnasy and Anette Kalnasy
All rights reserved.

No part of this book may be used or reproduced or distributed in any form, or by any means, or stored in a database or retrieval system, without the prior written permission of the authors.

Published by Luminary Media Group, an imprint of Pine Orchard, Inc.
Visit us on the internet at www.pineorchard.com

Printed in Canada.   10 9 8 7 6 5 4 3 2

ISBN 1-930580-12-6

Library of Congress Card Number: 00-110894

About the Authors

Kenneth (Kal) Kalnasy served with the First Marine Division in Korea, making the Inchon landing, fighting at the Chosin Reservoir (among the "Chosin Few"), participating in the withdrawal of the Marine forces and evacuation from Hungnam. He received three Purple Hearts.

When his son Steven asked about the Korean War, Kalnasy and his wife Anette answered by writing this book.

The authors live in Las Vegas and write children's stories. Their first children's book *Tales of the Pekingese Kids* will be released in the fall of 2001.

Photo and Cover Credits

Photographs courtesy of the Marine Corps University Research Archives. Reprinted by permission.

Special thanks to Kortegaard Engineering for assistance with the photos.

Front cover photo: First Marine Division takes to the road on withdrawal from Koto-ri. Hdqtrs. No. A-5358, Defense Dept. photo (Marine Corps), Sgt. F. C. Kerr.

Back cover photo, top right: U.S. Marines rest in the snow during move south from Koto-ri, December 8, 1950. Hdqtrs. No. A-5359, Defense Dept. photo (Marine Corps).

Back cover photo, lower left: Marines blast through a Chinese Communist road block south of Koto-ri. Enemy had blown bridge at a concrete power plant over mountain gorge. Engineers installed bridge and the column moves south toward the sea. Hdqtrs. No. A-5408, Defense Dept. photo (Marine Corps), Sgt. W. R. Keating.

Selection of this cover is due to suggestions of the Marines stationed at Kaneohe Bay, Hawaii, and the Aloah Chapter of the Chosin Few.

*Dedicated to not only the
Marines who fought and died
in Korea and Vietnam, but to
all Marines throughout
history and to Marines of
today and the future,
and to the
Chosin Few.*

CONTENTS

Introduction 1

Part I—Other Heroic Events

Boot Camp, Parris Island 5
Dynamite Comes in Small Packages 13
Welcome 19
Fish or Sink 23
Thou Shalt Not Steal 27
Now You See It, Now You Don't 31
AWOL with an Attitude 35
Exploding Latrine 39
I Believe 43
The Poker Game 47
The Great Bank Heist 51
Money to Burn 55
The Right of Every Marine 59
The Well 65
Torpedo Juice 69
Boston Hillbilly 73
Brass Balls 77
K-9 81
Suffer the Little Children to Come Unto Me 85
The Birthday Present 89
Halt! Who's There? 93
The Poggy Bait Caper 97
The Last of the Knights 101
Fear Is in the Eye of the Beholder 105
What Price Bravery 111
They Shall Come from the East 115

Part II—From the Beach to the Reservoir

Semper Fideles: Always Faithful 121
From the Beach to the Reservoir 125
Listing of Photographs 149

Introduction

This is a collection of short stories, compiled and narrated by the authors. Due to the fact that some of the participants may still be alive, the names have been changed. While most of these stories are true, some are tales of the authors' imagination. As to which individual stories fall into the realm of imagination, we leave that to the reader to decide.

All these stories take place in the years 1950-1951, mostly in a place called Korea. The authors have tried to approach the Korean War with some semblance of humor. Anyone who has been in a combat zone and seen or been involved in the horrors of war realize that in order to maintain one's sanity, one must reach out for humor.

Kal has managed to keep the memories of Korea buried in his mind for fifty years. He thanks his son Steven O. Kalnasy for urging the telling of these tales and, of course, for the writing of the poem "From the Beach to the Reservoir," which is also included in this book. The poem is a compilation of Kal's own activities during this period.

NOW, ON WITH THE STORIES.

PART I
OTHER HEROIC
EVENTS

Stories written
by Kal Kalnasy
with Anette Kalnasy

BOOT CAMP, PARRIS ISLAND

Boot camp can be a terrorizing experience, but none more so than having a drill sergeant with a speech impediment.

When the young Marines arrived at PI late in the afternoon, the bus doors opened and everyone was ordered out. Standing there, waiting, were three Marines: a staff sergeant, Larry Benson; a buck sergeant, Pete Ford; and a corporal, George Cappelli.

Sergeant Benson ordered everyone to drop his gear and stand at attention. There, standing in a line of what they thought was attention were "the sorriest-looking individuals to grace the island since its inception" (or so said Sergeant Benson).

Introductions were made. Corporal Cappelli then ordered the men to march to a building across the parking lot.

There, we were introduced to the barber. Barber? Hell, Delilah would have been proud of him.

After the haircuts (peaches had more fuzz) the recruits were herded into a line and issued their clothing. "Don't worry, one size fits all" was the comment made by the clerk.

Then everyone was marched over to a building that proved to be the barracks. This was to be their home for the next twelve weeks.

All the recruits were ordered to shower and dress. Lined up in front of the corporal was the sorriest sight imaginable.

Nothing fit. They looked like refugees from a ragmuffin convention. Caps were pulled down around the eyes (as there was no hair to hold the cap up).

"You people will stand at attention. You will not move unless I say to move. You people will salute anything that moves. You people are the lowest forms of humanity that I have had the displeasure to encounter in my whole life. I cannot understand why your mommas didn't drown you at birth."

Or at least that's what they thought they heard. For, you see, the corporal had a speech impediment. "You people" came out sounding like "yuz pebbles."

The first thought that crossed the recruits' minds was "MY GOD, I'VE LANDED IN HELL."

The Marine Corps philosophy where recruits are concerned is as follows:

Weeks 1 - 4: Mold them into human beings. In the state that they were in, they couldn't even qualify as humans.

Weeks 5 - 8: See if they could be molded into productive civilians.

Weeks 9 - 12: Make Marines out of them.

Boot Camp, Parris Island

Now, this is not about life in boot camp (as I was raised to believe that it was not nice to discuss horror stories around the innocent). No, these are a few tales of incidents that took place under a drill instructor that even God could not have understood.

In the Marine Corps, your Garand M-1 weapon was a rifle. Not a gun. In the army, it might be called "a gun," but not here. A gun was something found aboard war ships. Guns were those big things on ships, usually in the size of 5-inchers or 16-inchers or other such "swabbie" vernacular. Marines did not carry guns. Marines carried rifles.

The recruits were taught to field strip their rifle blindfolded or in the dark. They were taught the name of every piece. They were drilled in the understanding that this rifle was their tie to life or death. And therefore, this rifle should be given the honor of being called what it was. A RIFLE, not a gun.

The Marine was taught to love that rifle, to care for it, to clean and polish it, to sleep with it. For, while a girl might not be true to them, their rifle always would be.

There was a young recruit in the platoon who just couldn't get that concept implanted in his mind. After countless tirades by the corporal (At least, they sounded like tirades. I mean, who could understand?), the recruit was brought before Sergeant Ford. Sergeant Ford ordered the recruit to report to the parade ground at 0700 on Sunday morning.

Now, Sunday was a day at PI when visitors were allowed on the base. Not visitors for the recruits, mind you. (Recruits had not earned that privilege yet.)

So after arriving at the parade ground, the recruit was advised to take his rifle in his left hand. He was then ordered to unbutton his fly and take his "tool" in his right hand. He was then told that he would march down the parade ground for an hour, shouting at the top of his lungs:

"THIS IS MY RIFLE AND THIS IS MY GUN.

THIS ONE'S FOR WAR AND THIS ONE'S FOR FUN."

Needless to say, the one-man parade drew the attention of all the people in the vicinity of the spectacle. Many comments were heard from the bystanders.

"With a little tool like that, the balls must be the size of peas."

"Marines have brass balls. That little thing just couldn't support them."

And even from a little five-year-old: "Look, Mommy, he has a little pee-pee, just like mine."

While the young recruit felt humiliated, he did learn that in the Marine Corps, the M-1 was a rifle.

The recruits were lined up for inspection and one of the recruits was caught watching the corporal. Now, when a Marine is at attention, his eyes are riveted straight ahead.

The corporal marched up to the recruit, put his face no more than three inches from the recruit's, and said, "R chu n luv wit me boy?" (Or words to that effect.)

Boot Camp, Parris Island

"No, sir."

"Du I o chu money?"

"No, sir."

"Du I luk lik yoor momma?"

"No, sir."

"Den wat da hell chu wachin me for?"

PI, sitting on the ocean, was very humid and, because of the beach, there were millions of sand fleas. Next to sand fleas, regular fleas were wimps. Sand fleas were mean, ornery, and, it seemed, always hungry.

One afternoon, the recruits were marched down to the beach for what the corporal called "close order drill." All the drill was close as the recruits were less than two feet from each other. The order consisted mostly of "about face." Over and over, it was "about face."

Have you ever seen a corkscrew in operation? Well, after about fifty about-faces, he then ordered, "Forward, march." Have you ever tried to march forward when your ankles are buried twelve inches in the sand? Needless to say, the platoon landed face down in the sand.

As the recruits started to rise, the corporal screamed: "I DID NOT TELL YOU TO GET UP! THE ONLY ORDER I GAVE YOU WAS 'FORWARD, MARCH' AND UNLESS YOU ARE PLANNING ON MARCHING STRAIGHT TO HEAVEN, YOU WILL STAY IN THE PRONE POSITION!"

Now, while the sand wasn't that uncomfortable, the sand fleas taking you for a buffet were. After about two minutes, the corporal gave the order to stand and snap to attention. He then decided to hold an inspection of the rifles. Needless to say, there was sand in the barrels. The more rifles he inspected, the louder he screamed.

"THE MOST IMPORTANT THING IN LIFE YOU HAVE TO WORRY ABOUT IS YOUR RIFLE! THAT IS YOUR LIFE AND LOOK AT THE CONDITION IT IS IN! INSTEAD OF PROTECTING YOUR RIFLES, ALL YOU PEOPLE WORRIED ABOUT WAS PROTECTING YOUR FACE! WHY? I HAVE NO IDEA AS YOU ARE ALL UGLY AS SIN!"

While the tirade was going on, the recruits started to itch and scratch.

"WHO TOLD YOU TO MOVE?" screamed the corporal. "I didn't say you could move! YOU! Why are you moving when I didn't say anything about moving? Did you hear me say at ease?'

"No, sir," replied the recruit.

"Then why are you moving?"

"Sir, the sand fleas are biting. They're driving me crazy, sir."

"Son, don't worry about them driving you crazy. In your case, that would be a very short trip indeed," replied the corporal. "You will stand at attention and allow the sand fleas to bite. You may not know it, but they are eating. Would you deprive them of their supper?"

"No, sir, it's just that they seem to be taking a very long time to finish their dinner, sir."

"Are you being a smart ass, son? Or are you just naturally stupid? Do you get to have three square meals

Boot Camp, Parris Island

a day? They are taking their time with their dinner because you were not here this morning to feed them, and you were not here this afternoon to feed them. Perhaps I should bring you people down here three times a day, so that they can eat regularly. What do you people think?"

There were many more instances that required 150% of the recruits' attention to understand, but I don't want to beat the proverbial dead horse. I will mention one other incident in the lives of these particular recruits.

One week before graduation, (I should mention that this particular recruit platoon went on to become an honor platoon) orders came down from recruit command that all recruits must be allowed to see a movie. Now, PI had a beautiful outdoor movie facility. A lot like a drive-in but it also had a bleacher setup.

Staff Sergeant Benson notified the platoon that evening they would be going over to the movie facility to see a movie. So in the evening, the platoon was formed up and marched over to the movie facility. As they were arriving, the screen lit up and the movie started.

Staff Sergeant Benson called the platoon to a halt and said, "Do you people see the movie?"

The platoon responded with a loud "YES, SIR."

Staff Sergeant Benson then gave the order. "About face!" And the platoon was marched back to the barracks.

As Staff Sergeant Benson was later heard to remark:

"I followed the directive. They did see the movie. No one said how much of it they were to see."

I was very lucky to have met Corporal (later to be Sergeant) Cappelli. I also want you to know that he had a speaking voice of a movie actor. There wasn't one sign of any speech impediment.

I asked him one day, "Why, if you didn't have a speech problem, why did you let everyone think that you did?"

He replied, "One of the most difficult things to teach a recruit is to listen. In order to respond instantly to a command that may some day save his life or the lives of his buddies, he has to be taught to listen.

"By my speaking with an apparent speech impediment, the recruits are forced into listening. After all, to them, I was their father and mother and, most importantly, I was their guide to becoming a well-rounded Marine. I am also proud to say that I never had to wash anyone out of the Corps and most of the platoons that the three of us trained ended up as honor platoons."

DYNAMITE COMES IN SMALL PACKAGES

San Diego, California, June 1950.

Sitting in a bar that was pretty much considered to be an all-Navy drinking establishment, eight Marines were gathered at a table.

Among the Marines was a sergeant and this sergeant was huge. He was at least 6 feet 4 inches tall in his stocking feet. He must have weighted 260 pounds. (We'll call him Bob Merchant.)

When Bob had a few drinks in him, he was like Jack Dempsey and Primo Carnera rolled into one. He would have put John Henry to shame.

One of his other accomplishments was the fact that he liked to talk. I mean, he really liked to talk. And when Bob talked, everyone listened. It wasn't what Bob had to say that was so interesting. It was the fact that when Bob talked, you listened. And when Bob wanted a response, you responded.

A case in point: One afternoon, about a week before Bob had imbibed a few . . . oh hell, let's "call a spade a spade." He didn't have a few. What he did have damned near depleted the stock of one of the local establishments.

14 *Other Heroic Events*

So after about five hours of steady drinking, Bob decided that he would take a cab back to the base. As Bob said "good night" and left, we had a few more rounds and then decided to also return to base.

As we stepped outside into the sunlight, we were totally surprised to see Bob. There he was, standing there, talking. Now, knowing Bob's penchant for conversation, this didn't surprise us. What did surprise us was his audience.

Standing at the curb was a horse. That's right, I said *a horse*. This horse was hooked up to a wagon. Bob had his hand on the horse's shoulder and was just talking a blue streak.

We approached Bob and asked him what in the hell he was doing. (Now you must realize that we were very polite in our question.)

Bob looked at us with his bloodshot eyes and in a very serious tone responded.

"I have been talking to this bastard for a good hour and he still refuses to answer me. I want you to know that I am getting pissed off. If he doesn't say something pretty soon, I'm going to flatten the son of a bitch."

Before we could respond back, Bob said, "The hell with him."

He then drew back his fist and delivered a blow to the horse. He caught that horse right between the eyes. The horse's eyes glazed over and it fell to the ground.

Bob had killed it.

Dynamite Comes in Small Packages

But to get back to the Navy drinking establishment . . . there we were, drinking away, minding our own business when from the table next to us, a group of sailors were drinking and talking.

One of the sailors was heard to say, "Look at those stupid gyrenes. I guess they had to come in here to drink. After all, no self-respecting bar would allow those animals in, especially that huge gorilla. They must have sprung him from the zoo."

Bob's head popped up and as he started to reply, one of the other sailors was heard to say, "What do you expect? No human would ever join the Marines. They have to get their recruits from the zoo."

With that, Bob got up and walked over to the table of sailors and said, "How would you cream-puff swabbies like to go outside and settle this? I'll fight you all, one at a time or all together. It makes no difference. I'm going to take you one by one and shove your heads up your asses and make wagon wheels out of you."

As the sailors started to rise, one of them, a sailor who could have been no bigger than 5 feet 4 with his shoes on and weighing no more than 129 pounds soaking wet, said, "Guys, stay seated. It's my turn to tame the ape."

With that, the little sailor stood and walked out the door, heading for the alley. Bob followed.

A minute later, we could hear the racket coming from the alley and a few minutes later, the little sailor came back into the bar. He looked like a million bucks.

His uniform was spotless and there wasn't a hair out of place.

Throwing back our chairs, we raced outside. There, lying in the garbage, was Bob. He looked like he had been run through a meat grinder. His uniform was covered with blood. His face looked like he had been mauled by a herd of wild buffalo.

Exercising great caution, we flagged a cab, got Bob into it, and returned to the base.

The next day after Bob had sobered up, we asked him what had happened.

He replied, "I stepped outside and the next thing I knew, there seemed to be a hundred of these little swabbies all over me. Every time I raised my fists to hit him, things got all hazy. That little guy moved so fast I couldn't have hit him if I had a hundred fists. We have to go back to town today. I have to find that little bastard and congratulate him. If the Navy had ten more like him, we wouldn't need to go to war. All we'd have to do is turn those little bastards loose. It wouldn't take more than a few weeks for the enemy to surrender."

Was this story true?

All I'll say is that if Bob had existed, he would have said that he was going to live forever, that there wasn't a bullet made that would stop him.

Bob would have been partially right. Thirty-caliber bullets wouldn't have slowed him down, but a 50-caliber bullet would.

I know, for a fact, that if Bob had existed, he would have been awarded the Navy Cross. Of course, it would have been posthumously.

WELCOME

Not many civilians are aware of the tremendous rivalry that exists between the regular Marine and the Marine reservists.

Now, I know that you are thinking, "Why?"

Well, folks, it exists and sometimes that rivalry can cause some humorous incidents.

Camp Pendleton, August 1950.

With the advent of the Korean War, the Marine Corps was in a rush to rebuild the 1st Marine Division.

After World War II, the available Marine manpower had been reduced. There were barely enough Marines on active duty to make up a complete combat division. Congress, in its infinite wisdom, had decided that now, since we had won "the war to end all wars," there was no reason to keep the Navy's stepchild up to strength. Maintaining full-strength divisions meant less money available for congressional pet projects.

It wasn't that they had anything against Marines, although they probably didn't want their daughters to marry one. It was just that, if you were going to trim something, you selected the group that could make the least amount of noise. Politicians hate noise, especially if it is directed against them.

Well, when the Korean War broke out, there we were, undermanned.

The Marine Corps immediately started a recall of its reserve units. This was a wise thing to do as it had been barely five years since they were discharged.

A retraining area was set up at Pendleton and the Marines were told to get everything ready for the arrival of the reservists. Now, Marines being a fun-loving group by nature, decided to give our reserve cousins a very hearty and warm welcome.

The reserve area was clearly marked. The area was well policed with not a single cigarette butt in sight. The barracks' decks were waxed and shined. All was ship-shape for the arrival of our reserve cousins.

When they arrived, they were greeted with wild enthusiasm. Terms like "weekend warriors" were offered in good humor. Each barracks was flying the guidon of that particular unit. There was some discussion as to the merits of some of the reservists. The beer tents were full, and a glass or two or three were raised in camaraderie.

At about 2200, everyone retired to his barracks for a well-deserved rest.

But all the welcome had not been presented yet.

At about 0300, a group of shadowy figures approached the barracks of one of the reserve companies.

Quietly, something that looked like a 50-caliber machine gun was set up at each entrance to the barracks.

Welcome

At the stroke of 0330, the machine guns opened up on the barracks where the sleeping reserve Marines were. Spotlights were turned on, and voices that sounded oriental were heard screaming.

To say that the reservists leaped out of their bunks was an understatement.

Needless to say, the welcome that had been provided for them seemed to be totally unappreciated.

Now, please don't think that we did not like our reservists, far from it. It was just our way of saying, "Welcome."

FISH OR SINK

Osaka, Japan, August 1950.

We had arrived in Japan.

The work of preparing for a major amphibious landing was not only time-consuming, but also boring as hell.

After three days, we were granted liberty. We were all warned to discuss nothing about what was happening in the staging area. Six or seven of us decided to go into town and see what we could find.

Now remember, this was 1950, just five years after the surrender of Japan. In the minds of many of the Japanese, we were still considered the enemy. They hadn't developed the Toyota yet and still hadn't devised their plan of buying the good old U.S. of A.

Outside of Osaka was a small village, clustered around a small lake. The only industry in the village was fishing.

One of the Marines with us, Peter Barranca, had grown up in Maine and was an avid fisherman. Upon seeing the lake and all the fishing boats, Peter decided that he would like to fish.

We approached a group of men sitting in a small park. Peter asked if anyone spoke English. One of the villagers nodded yes.

Peter then asked if it would be possible to rent one of the boats and do some fishing. He explained that if any fish were caught, they would be given to the villagers.

In broken English, the villager responded: "We do not like you. You are all butchers and evil demons, and we do not want you in our village."

Peter turned beet red and reached out and grabbed the villager and started to shake him.

At that, all the villagers present rose up and started to move towards us. Remembering our orders about no fraternizing with the locals and also realizing that this could be big trouble, Peter let go of the man.

He said, "We came to your village to enjoy a peaceful day. Instead, we find that you people stink worse than your goddamned honey buckets. As far as I'm concerned, you can shove your damned boats up your asses. Remember one thing, assholes, you started the goddamned war and we finished it. I can't tell you how much pleasure we got in kicking your slant-eyed asses."

As some of the villagers bent down to pick up some stones that we figured they intended to throw at us, we beat a hasty retreat.

We left the village and returned to Osaka, where the people were much friendlier (probably future Toyota workers). We found a bar and proceeded to do what Marines do best: drink.

Fish or Sink

The more we drank, the more pissed off Peter got. He decided that he would get even with those little yellow bastards. After returning to the base and getting a good night's sleep, Peter seemed to have forgotten the incident at the fishing village.

Three days later, Peter, with a smile on his face, said: "How would you guys like to join me in a visit to the village? I have finally figured out how to get even with those rotten bastards."

Now, as Peter was one of our friends, we figured that the least we could do was to help him with his plan, no matter what it was.

That night, eight of us snuck off the base and returned to the village. We were dressed in combat fatigues with our faces blackened, and following Peter, we crept up to the area where all the boats were moored.

Crawling aboard, we pulled the plug on the boat and then watched as it sank beneath the water.

Getting into the spirit of the raid, we proceeded to pull the plugs on the rest of the boats. The raid was very successful—we managed to sink 123 fishing boats.

It probably went into the books as the most devastating naval loss in history, second only to the destruction of the Spanish Armada. Feeling the glow of a successful operation, we retired to a friendly watering hole in Osaka.

Of course, not being familiar with the statute of limitations as it refers to a foreign country, I totally deny any participation in the raid.

Now, if the incident had happened, I am quite sure that Peter would have gone into some occupation involving destruction.

Last week, I was talking to a construction worker here in Las Vegas and he mentioned that he had just come from a retirement party for the best damned implosion expert to have ever destroyed a building.

"You know, in the business, Peter is a legend," he said.

I was about to ask the last name of Peter, but I decided maybe I really didn't want to know that.

THOU SHALT NOT STEAL

Somewhere in Japan, 1950.

Being a history buff, when I arrived in Japan, I heard about a Buddha. I don't mean any Buddha. I mean one of the largest in the world.

So a week or so after my arrival in Japan, I went on a visit to the sight of this Buddha. Let me tell you, it impressed the hell out of me. I didn't realize that they made idols that big.

It was located in a Buddhist temple and, when I entered the temple, I was stunned by the sight of the jewel set in the head of that Buddha. I just stood there in total amazement. Never had I seen anything that large or more beautiful.

When I returned to the base, I just couldn't stop talking about it. After listening to me rave about the Buddha, a group of my buddies decided that they would like to see it also.

That weekend, a group of us returned to the temple and I could see the amazement on their faces. After we got back to the base, we continued to comment on the idol and the jewel in its forehead.

The next comment that I heard was, "You know, we are here to learn everything we can about camouflage. If we could sneak into the temple and remove the jewel from its head without anyone knowing that we were there, that would be a fantastic coup."

"We do plan on giving it back, I hope. I sure wouldn't want to get into trouble."

"Of course, we'll give it back. What do you think we are, a bunch of crooks?"

We decided that we would plan the raid and take the jewel as prisoner. We felt that the Japanese instructors would be pleased if we could pull it off.

As another safeguard, we decided that we would outline in total detail what we were planning. A copy of the plan would be placed in the colonel's mail and also in the box of the chief Japanese instructor. To be sure that there would be no warning, we would leave the information right as we were ready to leave. We felt that as this was the weekend, no one would open the envelopes until after we had conducted the raid.

We sent one man back to make a detailed drawing of the compound and the temple. We also surveyed all the surrounding area.

Saturday evening, we left for the temple. We were dressed to blend in with the shrubs and foliage of the surrounding area.

Slowly and cautiously, we approached the temple. Still no sign of any guards or monks. We carefully entered the temple.

And there, straight ahead of us was the idol.

Thou Shalt Not Steal 29

The jewel in the forehead glowed from the light cast by the torches ensconced on the walls. The flickering lights gave off an eerie glow. The eyes of the idol appeared to be watching us. As we moved towards it, we fanned out. The eyes seemed to follow us, no matter the position we were in at any given time.

Then, as we arrived at the base of the idol and prepared to ascend the steps to start the climb towards the idol's head, we heard a noise that sounded like the soft brush of the leaves of a tree, caused by a gentle breeze.

Looking around, there before our startled eyes were monks. They were positioned along the wall, completely surrounding us. They seemed to have oozed out of the walls.

We immediately did the proper thing. Bowing and kowtowing to the idol, we slowly backed out of the temple.

Arriving back at the base, we realized that we had been given a lesson in camouflage that we would never forget.

If this really happened, the lesson to be learned from this was twofold:

1. Never invade a person's place of worship.

2. No matter how good you are in whatever you are doing, there is always someone who is a little better.

NOW YOU SEE IT, NOW YOU DON'T

Kobe, Japan, August 1950.

There we were, loading the good ol' Japanese LST QO73 . . . day after day after day.

Headquarters, in their infinite wisdom, decided that in order to maintain high security all Marines were confined to the loading area. In our case, it was the glorious old rust bucket QO73.

Every day we watched as the Japanese workmen were transported by truck off the base, only to return the following morning.

Someone had the brilliant idea for us to climb into the back of the truck, dressed in our fatigues with our Class-A uniforms underneath. Late the next afternoon, as the workmen got ready to leave the base, six of us climbed aboard and hid under the gear in the rear of the truck.

We were safely able to get through the checkpoint and after the truck left the dock area, we climbed off, hid our fatigues, and were all prepared to sample the nightlife. As luck would have it, the cab driver that we hailed was more than willing to take us to the nearest Japanese fun house.

Mamma-san greeted us with open arms. And I do mean that literally. But being young and very eager, we soon convinced her to bring out her daughters.

It was absolutely amazing how many daughters she seemed to have. The astonishing thing was that there had to be at least fifteen of them the same age.

Now to tell the truth, I kind of had my doubts. I mean, the idea that she had fifteen daughters born at the same time was kind of farfetched. Of course, being very trusting souls, my buddies and I were more than willing to give her the benefit of the doubt.

And of course, after careful scrutiny, I could see where this might be so. I mean, she looked like a mean old junkyard dog. So I suppose she could have had an exceptionally large litter.

Mamma-san assured us that the girls were clean family girls and, of course, they were all virgins. And as I said before, I was very trusting so I had no reason to doubt her.

I will say one thing, though: They were the damnedest quick learners I have ever come across to this day. I mean, they learned things before I even had a chance to teach them. They gave new meaning to the expression "around the world."

As dawn was breaking, we crept into the back of the truck that was bringing the workman on to the base. (I want to say that we could not have had a better time at Mamma-san's establishment if we had owned it ourselves.)

Now You See It, Now You Don't 33

Every afternoon for the next four days, we were able to get off base and return to Mamma-san's house to continue the education of her wonderful daughters. And of course, we were helping her to reach a higher standard of living.

On the morning of the fifth day, we once again arrived back at the docks and received a terrible shock. The good old QO73 was gone!

The first thing that crossed our minds was that we were in deep shit. If the ship had sailed, we were guilty of desertion.

What in the hell were we to do?

We made discrete inquiries and found out that the LST was anchored out in the harbor. It had completed its loading and was prepared to sail.

Quickly, we hired a Japanese fishing boat to take us out to the ship. After arriving, we climbed aboard the fantail. Creeping aboard, we were able to climb down the ladder to our bunks.

After changing clothes, we nonchalantly went up on deck. There, lounging in a deck chair we saw the skipper.

We walked up to him, saluted, and said, "Good morning, Skipper. What are the orders of the day?"

Looking at us with fire in his eyes, he replied, "Where the hell have you assholes been?"

"I'm sorry, Skipper, it seems that we overslept and didn't hear reveille."

"You mean that you were sleeping so soundly that you never heard anything?"

"That's right, sir. We worked so hard loading yesterday that I guess that we were just exhausted. We apologize, sir. We promise that it will never happen again."

"You goddamned right it won't happen again. Let me bring you up to date. First, the company has been transferred to another ship. This happened late yesterday afternoon. Second, since none of you were aboard ship, you didn't know that. Third, you were spotted sneaking back on to the base. Fourth, I decided to wait here to greet you. Fifth, you goddamned yard birds are in deep shit. Sixth, you are all on report and will report to me in my office which, by the way, is that ship over there tied up at the pier. Seventh, you can all kiss your ass good-bye because it now belongs to me. Eighth, get the hell out of my sight before I have you shot for desertion."

We returned to shore and at 1000 hours, we were standing before the Colonel.

He looked at us and said, "The rest of the outfit will have two days liberty. You clowns will stand guard duty. I would have your asses thrown into the brig, but I figure, what the hell, you're probably all going to get your asses shot off, anyway."

Did any of this happen?

Well, who's to say? Not me.

I will say one thing: If it had happened, I would have been glad that the Colonel was Chesty Puller.

AWOL WITH AN ATTITUDE

Army Air Base, South Korea, 1951.

After the Reservoir, the 1st Marine division was sent to Masan, Korea.

The object was to bring the division back up to strength. The casualty rate had been extremely high. For some reason, the X corps figured that they would take Eleanor Roosevelt's suggestion to heart and keep us isolated.

She had made the comment (and I do not recall the exact words) that, in essence, Marines coming out of combat were like wild animals and the rest of the civilized world should not be exposed to them.

She may have been right. I know that as keyed up as we were, I would not have been too happy associating with us. But then, I wasn't too bright as evidenced by the fact that I was in Korea.

Anyway, one day six marines decided that it would be a fantastic idea if they could see how the other half lived. So that night, the six Marines left the compound and headed towards Pusan.

36   *Other Heroic Events*

Just outside of Pusan was an airbase—we'll call it K-9. Arriving at the airbase, the six infiltrated the base and liberated six officers' uniforms. Then, they procured billeting in the officers' area.

Now, I wouldn't want to say that they went overboard, but they did make full use of the facilities that were available. Their stay lasted for three days. Then deciding that discretion was the better part of valor, they left the happy confines of K-9 and headed for Pusan.

Arriving in Pusan, the happy and AWOL six decided to see just how much beer and mountain juice they could drink. Of course, with every drink their pleasant and warm personalities seemed to rise to the forefront.

Now, like any peaceful and gregarious Marine would do, they decided to see what kind of physical shape our allies were in. With each round of the nectar of the gods they consumed, they challenged the various contingents of our United Nations troops who were also interested in tasting the various types of alcoholic beverages being offered by the bartenders.

Knowing full well that it was not wise to consume large quantities of these beverages without some form of physical activity to relieve the body of some of the calories, they suggested to the various contingents such as the Turks and the Black Watch Scots that they might want to share in this exercise.

Not speaking English with any proficiency, our foreign allies were more than willing to assist us in our endeavors.

AWOL with an Attitude

This period of camaraderie lasted four days. About that time, the six realizing that they could be in serious trouble decided that the best thing that they could do was to bring back to the camp at Masan a peace offering. While the thought was good, the opportunities for such an offering seemed to be few and far between.

But then Lady Luck decided to intervene in the lives of these magnificent Marines.

While strolling along the docks, they noticed that a large supply ship had docked. After making discrete inquiries, they found out that the ship was loaded from stem to stern with beer. Remembering the time-honored tradition that said any Marine in a combat zone was entitled to the consumption of two cans of beer and, as their inquiries had elicited the facts that the beer was destined for delivery to various Army camps, realizing that obviously this had to have been an oversight, they decided that the best thing that they could do was to liberate a small quantity for their thirsty foxhole buddies back at camp.

Now as luck would have it, parked in front of a building that looked like it was some kind of regimental headquarters was a beautiful canvas-covered 6-by-6 truck. Not only was the truck parked there all by itself, but also the gods had arranged for the keys to be in the ignition.

Realizing that it would never do to refuse to accept this gift from the gods, they promptly borrowed the truck and drove to the supply ship. There, they proceeded to sign the name of a fictitious Army colonel, then requisitioned 640 cases of this marvelous brew.

They immediately proceeded to drive back to Masan with their peace offering.

While they were welcomed with open arms, they were still brought before Chesty Puller. Being a very stern and go-by-the-book commander, Chesty assigned the wayward six to the tasks of digging new latrines.

Two days later, four Army MPs arrived at the base prepared to take into custody the wayward six. But, as luck would have it, Chesty had just assigned the six to a recon patrol.

Well, I will not swear to the truth of the above story but taking into consideration the healthy outlook that our Marines were always able to manifest and the fact that if the incident had taken place, Chesty would have acted as the author described.

Semper Fi, Chesty.

EXPLODING LATRINE

Now, one of the Marines who had been involved in the great beer caper, after digging about a dozen latrines, decided that Chesty had been grossly unfair. After all, he reasoned, didn't he help bring back all that glorious beer?

The more he thought about it, the more he felt that he had to get even.

He thought and thought. It wasn't getting even that was so important. It was the method. It had to be something appropriate, something that would fit the punishment.

He thought and he thought for days on end. Idea after idea crossed his feverish brain. Each was discarded as either too dangerous or too simple. After all, he didn't want to hurt or kill Chesty. He just wanted to get even.

He couldn't sleep. He had difficulty eating. No touch football. No letters home. He just sat there and seemed to be brooding. And then, like a glorious revelation from heaven, he had the answer.

For the next two weeks, he seemed to be another Marine—smiling, laughing, and joking around. He surprised everyone, when after his punishment was over,

40   *Other Heroic Events*

he volunteered to dig more latrines. The sergeant thought about calling division and requesting a visit from the division shrink, but then figured, what the hell, if he wanted to dig, let him.

And dig he did.

He brought the art of latrine digging to new heights. You could have used a T-square to measure the holes. Each was eight feet long, four feet wide, and adding new refinements to the art, each was exactly eight feet deep. You would have sworn that a construction engineer had dug them.

The seats of the latrine were hand-sanded by him, allowing for no possibility of any splinters. They were truly a work of art.

He went so far as to dig a special one for the officers with a hand-painted sign over one that read: "Colonel Chesty Puller. Private." It was truly a wondrous thing to behold.

He had even gone so far as to buy some wool from one of the farmers and had the farmer's wife make a woolen toilet seat cover. For the lid, (yes, he did make a lid), on the inside of the lid, he had painted an emblem of a colonel's eagle.

He insisted that Chesty come and view his masterpiece. Chesty, wanting to reward such diligence, thanked him and formally removed him from latrine duty.

One night, as Chesty sat on his glorious throne in magnificent splendor, the Marine crept up to the rear of

Exploding Latrine 41

the latrine, pulled out a grenade, pulled the pin, and through a small flap in the tent that he had previously put there, reached in, and dropped the grenade down the adjoining hole.

There was a tremendous explosion.

Needless to say, there was sh-t all over the place. Chesty hadn't been harmed, since the Marine had removed most of the powder from the charge. But it was a toss-up as to what had arrived in heaven first: the curses from Chesty or the flying sh-t.

As they marched the private off to the stockade, the smile on his face would have nominated him for sainthood.

After twenty-four hours in the stockade, the Marine was released. Chesty informed him that, after due consideration, he had decided to drop the charges. He figured that the Marine would probably just figure out another devious way to get even.

After the Marine left Chesty's tent, Chesty was heard to say: "The planning and execution of the incident was absolutely brilliant. Please make sure that you remind me to promote him back to corporal as soon as possible." Then he started to laugh. "This would have been something that I would have pulled when I was at VMI."

Did this really happen? Who knows for sure? After all, you would have had to have been there.

All I will say is that for quite awhile, Chesty walked

around with a sh-t eating grin on his face. He also never used the officers' latrine again, electing, instead, to use the enlisted men's latrine.

Do you think that he felt it was safer?

You know, Chesty was nobody's fool.

I BELIEVE

Strange things happen when one is in a war zone. We fret and worry about what is happening back home. We sit and think, "Boy, I wonder what my wife is doing" or "I wonder what my girlfriend is doing" and sometimes we wonder what they both are doing.

We had a young Marine in our company who had been on embassy duty in Manila. He had been there from April 1950 until the Korean War broke out.

With the need for the presence of Marines in Korea as soon as possible, he was landed in Pusan, Korea, on August 3, 1950. Unlike many of us, he had not been home since March of 1950.

He had married a young girl from his hometown of Padukah, Kentucky, and had had exactly four days for his wedding and honeymoon. Needless to say, being very young and very much in love, he was concerned with the welfare of his young wife.

Now, in one of the quirks of the war, the young Marine had not been receiving any mail from home. The Fleet post office, in its infinite wisdom, kept sending his mail to Manila. He had not received any mail at all until February of 1951. Imagine his surprise when he received his first letter from his young wife and in the letter, she told him that the day before yesterday, he became the proud father of a baby boy.

Now the Marine, like all young fathers, started beaming with pride. Then, he stopped and started counting back on his fingers. She said in her letter that the day before yesterday he had become a father. After making discrete inquiries, he found that the average delivery time from the States to the unit was six days. That meant that the baby was about two weeks old, allowing for a slow delivery.

A quick count meant that his young wife must have gotten pregnant in May or June of 1950. But he hadn't been home since March of 1950 which meant that it was an 11-month pregnancy, or something was radically wrong.

He loved his wife and really and truly wanted to believe that the baby was his. For two weeks, he kept walking around saying to himself, "I believe, I believe."

Everyone could see that something was bothering the boy but, as he had never confided in anyone, they did not know the problem so they could not help. Finally, the company sergeant paid a call on the chaplain and asked the padre if he could possibly find out what was bothering the young Marine.

The chaplain sent for the young Marine and when he arrived at the chaplain's tent, the chaplain started to question him.

"Son what seems to be the matter? Your sergeant

I Believe   45

tells me that you have been walking around muttering to yourself repeating over and over the phrase 'I believe.' Son, what is it that you want to believe?"

The young Marine, while not wanting to mention his troubles, decided that he could trust the chaplain. He then proceeded to explain the letter that he had received telling him that he was a father, then explained the time frame involved.

The chaplain decided that the only way this was going to be settled was to contact the wife of the Marine.

Asking the Marine to wait, the chaplain went to the colonel and explained the problem and requested permission to call the young wife and get the whole story. He figured that the Marine would not be able to perform his duties and could endanger both himself and also his platoon. The colonel agreed and notified the company clerk to attempt to make contact with the wife of the Marine.

The chaplain notified the Marine that shortly they would have a phone line established to his wife and he would be allowed to speak to her. Six hours later, the young Marine was called to the communication tent to speak to her.

As the conversation progressed, a huge smile appeared on the face of the Marine. And then everyone heard him say: "Honey, I told everyone that I believed and I am sure glad that I did."

After hanging up, he explained that the letter was one that had been returned from Manila and she had just resent it, forgetting to upgrade the time sequence.

The young Marine had become a father in December—exactly nine months from the date of their last meeting.

I will tell everyone that this story is definitely true. And you do have to admire the love of the young Marine.

THE POKER GAME

It seems that when a boy joins the Marine Corps (I can't vouch for the women Marines), one of the first types of recreation he learns is poker.

Sometimes I think that the concept of the Marine Corps came during a poker game in Tun's tavern. It seems to be in our blood. This should not be a surprise to anyone. After all, a Marine loves to gamble. If he didn't, why else would he be in the Marine Corps?

The following story concerns poker, or at least takes place at a poker game.

In a previous story "The Exploding Latrine," you were introduced to the Marine who built the elaborate latrine. Chesty had him confined to the stockade (field brig) for a few days. After that, he was released and given his stripes back. Now, you would think that would have been the end of the story. Well, unfortunately, that was not the case.

The young Marine in question was known to hoist a few drinks too many. And when he did, his mind seemed to assume a life of its own.

About a month after the latrine issue, he decided

47

that he really didn't like officers and he really should do something about it. It had to be something spectacular. It had to be more of a spectacle than the exploding latrine.

But what?

His feverishly demonic mind kept coming up with various plans only to have them discarded for various reasons. Some were too mild; some were too dangerous. Some were impossible to do without killing someone. And while he had a warped mind, he wasn't homicidal.

For two weeks, he gave the matter a lot of thought. But then, it came to him: POKER.

Poker was the answer.

In January, the outfit had set up at Masan. There was no sign that we were to return to combat until the regiment was brought up to strength. In every tent, there was a poker game going on. After all, wasn't poker the relaxation of choice?

The men had been paid, and there was no doubt MacArthur's promise that all Americans would be home by Christmas had been a lot of bull sh-t. We were here. And, wonder of all wonders, we were alive.

In the officers' tent, a poker game was also taking place.

Now, these games were continuous events, be they enlisted or officer. If there was a respite in the battle, there was a poker game.

The game had been going on for almost three days. And while the game continued, the eyes of the officers

The Poker Game 49

weren't functioning too well. It was about 0100 and the betting was going along nicely when into the tent came charging our disgruntled young Marine.

All the officers looked up and there before their eyes was this spectacle of horror.

Standing at the tent flap door was this wild-eyed Marine screaming "I HATE OFFICERS. I HATE ALL OFFICERS. I AM GOING TO DO THE CORPS A BIG FAVOR AND KILL ALL YOU ASSHOLES."

With that, he reached into his pocket, pulled out a hand grenade, pulled the pin, and tossed it into the middle of the table. Then, he started to laugh like a wild hyena.

For a second or two, there was no movement at all in the tent. And then the officers went crazy, trying to get out of the tent. They couldn't go toward the entrance because the Marine had another grenade in his hand and you could see that the pin had been pulled. There was only one normal exit from the tent and, of course, there was even more danger there.

In a matter of seconds, out came the bayonets and seven frantic officers were desperately slashing at the tent walls, trying to cut their way out. In the meantime, the Marine was now down on his knees, laughing so hard, tears were running down his cheeks.

For you see, he had taken out all the powder in both grenades.

While Chesty hadn't been there, he was still the one to set the punishment. The young Marine was subdued and sent back to the States. He spent almost six months in the lock ward of the Naval hospital at Great Lakes.

He was later discharged from the Marines, honorably, I might add, and went on to a brilliant career in show business, including a comedy act that did quite well in television.

I will not identify him as he is still alive and occasionally makes guest appearances on TV.

THE GREAT BANK HEIST

Tokyo, 1951.

Tokyo Bank's main branch opened its doors at 0900. The officers had hardly settled in when, into the bank, walked three men in United States uniforms.

They announced that they were from the Occupation Forces Finance Division. They began by telling the bank's head teller that they had been notified that there were large discrepancies in the bank's books and ordered all the bank books be brought to them, so they could start an internal audit.

For three days, the military audit team went over the books.

The morning of the fourth day, the auditors arrived accompanied by four MPs. They notified the bank that large irregularities had been discovered in the books and said that the bank would be closed until further notice. The police would be sent and whoever was responsible would be prosecuted.

They also informed the bank officials that all the books and all the money would be removed to U.S. Army headquarters for safekeeping. The auditors and the MPs then proceeded to load up all the money from the vault into a large truck. After all the money and books were removed, they proceeded to place a padlock on the bank. They got into their vehicles and drove away.

The next day, customers were lined up outside the bank, waiting to get in. When no one arrived to open the bank, they called the police. That is when they discovered that the bank had been robbed.

A massive investigation was started, but no clue as to the identity of the crooks was found.

The Japanese government was in a panic. Not only were all the bank funds removed, but also the officers who had allowed the phony auditors access to the books and who had helped the crooks load the money into the van were shamed and totally humiliated.

The officers of the bank, following Japanese custom, committed hari-kari.

The hunt for the thieves continued, but no clues as to their identity were uncovered. The United States Military Occupation Forces replaced the money. The hunt for the crooks continued, but after six months there was still no sign of who the crooks were.

Five military police were getting ready to be rotated back to the U.S. This was not all milk and honey. Before they were rotated, they were required to have physicals. They had to turn in all weapons assigned to them by the M.P. Battalion. So, they were basically on TAD.

While they were at the medical center, the company was notified that there would be an inspection of the

The Great Bank Heist 53

barracks. The first sergeant, while doing a walk-through of the barracks prior to the inspection, noticed that the bunks of the men scheduled to be rotated seemed to be in a little bit of disarray. The bunks were definitely not up to military standards.

Knowing that the men were to be processed out the following day and not wanting any bad marks entered into their records, the sarge decided that he would make their bunks as ship-shape as possible.

As the sarge was trying to smooth out the wrinkles and bumps in the bunk, he noticed that the problem seemed to be in the mattress cover. No matter how hard he tried to smooth it out, the more he realized that the mattress seemed to be out of shape.

Deciding that the best solution would be to replace the mattress, he stripped off the mattress cover and discovered that the mattress had a tear in it. As he picked up the mattress, he saw a tip of a bill which seemed to be inside a slit in the mattress. He called for the officer-of-the-day.

When the officer arrived, he showed him what he had discovered. The officer took a penknife and proceeded to cut a small slit in the mattress and observed that the whole interior of the mattress seemed to be filled with money.

He contacted headquarters, and they decided that they would cancel the inspection. They put the bunk back the way they had found it and placed a watch on the barracks.

The next day, the five men who were to be rotated

54

Other Heroic Events

started to pack their gear. They were all seen removing money from their mattresses. As they were about to board the bus that would transfer them to the plane for the U.S., MPs arrived and took them into custody.

You guessed it—these were the phony auditors.

In the six months since the robbery, they had purchased various souvenirs and proceeded to fill them with the money they had stolen from the bank. They were all charged with robbery and also charged with causing the death of the bank officials who had committed hari-kari.

As to whether this actually happened, I would ask you to procure copies of the Japanese newspapers for that period and do your own research.

But if it had happened, you would have to give an "A" for outstanding planning and another "A" for the bold execution of the operation.

What a future they would have had in battle planning.

MONEY TO BURN

For six days, we sailed back and forth while the beach at Wonson was cleared. The North Koreans, expecting an invasion, had mined the harbor and the beach. Their gun emplacements covered every inch of the beach. If we had had to storm the beach, I doubt if many of us would have survived.

As luck would have it, a ROK division swept in and took the city.

Anyway, near the North Korean capital of Pyongyang, a supply depot was set up. Sometimes some officers can do stupid things (not Marine officers, of course) and make tactical errors that can cause needless loss of troops.

Knowing that the North Koreans were starving and wanting to protect the supplies (much of which was food) the colonel, commanding the army supply center, established a perimeter guard around the food.

The idea was good. The planning was terrible.

The men were ordered to dig their foxholes in an encircling perimeter. Unfortunately, the foxholes were fifty yards apart. Attracted to the food, the North Korean unit infiltrated the perimeter and managed to bayonet most of the army troops in their sleeping bags.

When news reached the first Marine division, we were rushed to the area by train. Arriving in Pyongyang, we were faced with the impossible task of identifying the perpetrators responsible for the slaughter.

Amazingly, everyone we encountered was a civilian. Isn't it amazing how swiftly the enemy can disappear from sight? (We saw the same thing in Vietnam.)

Under the Geneva Convention, civilians cannot be held responsible for the actions of the military forces of their country unless, of course, they were the ones giving the orders.

Retaliation was required, but retaliation against who?

Now, as we have learned from personal experience, the civilians were mostly interested in their own welfare. With this in mind, the Marines decided to teach the population both civilian and military (if there were any military) a lesson in revenge.

As Pyongyang was the capital of North Korea, it had many institutions in the city, including at least eleven banks.

An assault was mounted against each and every bank in the city. All moneys and valuables were rounded up. Brought up were 3.5 rocket launchers and the bank vaults were blown. (Willie Sutton, eat your heart out.) All the money and all the valuables were piled high in the center of the city. As William Buckley would have said, "Billions and billions and billions of dollars were added to the pile."

There were deeds to property. There were Russian war bonds. There was paper money of all denominations and all nationalities. There was, of course, a few thousand dollars in U.S. currency. (Being honest Marines, I have no doubt in my mind that the U.S. currency was also added to the pile.)

All the civilians that could be found were herded into the area, surrounding the huge pile of valuables. Fifty-caliber machine guns were placed in a circle around the pile and the civilians. Then, a flame thrower was used to set fire to the money pyre.

The spectators were screaming in anguish as the bonfire got bigger and bigger. Many of them tried to rescue some of the money. But as each attempt was made, the machine guns opened up. The fire was not directed at the civilians but a few feet above their heads or a few feet in front of them.

When the pile was completely burned, the Marines left.

Revenge can be sweet and I think that a fine lesson was learned by all: Monetary death can be as fatal as mortal death.

Way to go, Marines. *Semper Fi.*

THE RIGHT
OF EVERY MARINE

Korea, 1951, Front Lines.

Korea could be a bitch.

There we were, dug in, waiting for an attack at any moment. Regiment on 50% alert.

We had many alerts, expecting the Chinese to start another one of their bugle calls, signaling another human wave charge.

I used to wonder what would give out first: the Chinese with its massive population or our bullets coming from our prolific arms suppliers?

Anyway, one of the God-given rights of a Marine is the right to scrounge. Being very low on the military supply chain required a Marine to supplement his barely adequate supplies with whatever God provided or whatever he could find that wasn't nailed down. Of course, a good Marine also carried a pry-bar to assist in the liberation of those items that were nailed down.

One morning, notice came down from Division that we could stand down. The threat of an attack by Chinese troops in our perimeter had been greatly reduced. It seemed that the Chinese army needed some easier

60 *Other Heroic Events*

targets and were concentrating on South Korean positions.

No sooner had these orders come down from Division, then down the road came a large convoy of trucks. Behind our position was a road and across that road was a very large open area. These trucks pulled into that area and soldiers proceeded to set up a camp. Tents went up in perfect order, each one being thirty feet apart. Bulldozers proceeded to lay out streets. Hell, they even put up street signs. Mess tents were set up. Supply tents were set up. Latrines were dug in very precise positions. Then, would you believe they started to install razor-wire fencing all around the perimeter of their pretty camp?

Then, wonder of wonders. Supply trucks started to roll up. These trucks were loaded with all kind of goodies.

We sauntered over to give these newcomers a warm welcome. But, would you believe it? We were refused entrance. This camp was for Army personnel only.

Now, that is not the way to treat Marines . . . especially such honest and forthright Marines like us.

But wanting to be helpful, we decided that we should assist them in their security efforts. After all, we didn't want them to wake up in their cute little cots, step outside in their jammies, and find that the Chinese had infiltrated and stolen some of their precious supplies.

We decided to test their security systems.

That night, twenty-one Marines, wearing camouflage and night paint on our faces, crept across

The Right of Every Marine   61

the road. Silently, we cut an access hole into their razor-wire fence. Leaving one Marine to act as a rear guard, we snaked through their perimeter guard positions.

Once inside, we proceeded to check the inventory in their supply trucks. We found one loaded with K-rations and proceeded to resupply our needs. Two trucks later, we struck gold.

Would you believe we had found a truck loaded with case after case of canned beer?

Now, obviously, we realized that they were probably preparing to throw a party and invite us over. Feeling that would be an awful lot of work for our new neighbors, we decided to help them in the distribution of such fine supplies. We made seven different trips to those two supply trucks.

I do have to apologize. It wasn't until later that I realized that we had forgotten to leave a thank-you note. But I figured that, what the hell, we could leave one on our next visit.

That next morning, we did notice there seemed to be a lot of commotion over at our neighbors. We figured that they were probably thrilled that we had assisted them in the disposal of such fine supplies. After all, they were a resupply depot.

We were so pleased with the hospitality that they had shown us that we decided it would only be neighborly if we paid them a return visit. I mean, how often does one encounter such generous neighbors?

That night, we once again penetrated their perimeter.

We did find that they had improved their security quite a bit. This pleased us to no end. I mean how often does one see one's security suggestions implemented so swiftly?

We approached the supply area and noticed that they had moved everything. We figured that they really wanted their security system checked out so we deployed scouts to see where all the goodies had been stored. After about fifteen minutes, word came that the supply trucks had been located.

Wanting to finish the security test as rapidly as possible, I crawled into the interior of one of the supply trucks and proceeded to hand out the cases of goodies inside.

Everything was going well when one of the men outside said, "Watch it. Here comes a guard."

After being informed that the guard was too close for me to effectively remove myself from the truck's interior, I decided that this might be the time to test the reactions of their sentries. Sitting down on a case of goods in the truck, I drew my .45-automatic and waited.

Now, not wanting to exert too much energy, I propped my arm on a case in front of me and with the .45 in plain sight, I waited for the sentry to discover me.

I did not have a long wait.

The flap of the truck was moved, and there stood a sentry with his flashlight on and shining directly into the truck's interior. I knew that he could not possibly fail to see me.

I waited for his greeting.

Looking back on the incident, I now realize that this was not a good test for him. I doubt if he was able to see anything except the .45 which, of course, was aimed directly at him at eye level.

It was at that time I heard a voice say, "Do you see anyone in that truck?"

Knowing that must be the sergeant of the guard, I waited for the guard's response.

I was not disappointed.

I heard the guard say, "No, sir, there is no one in this truck."

The guard then dropped the flap, and I heard him leave.

Not wanting to put the poor guard in a difficult position and figuring as soon as he went to his tent and changed his shorts that he probably would want to return with some of his buddies and extend a formal welcome, I decided that it probably was best if I returned to my own position. With that, I beat a hasty retreat.

Now I know that many of you will want to know if this story was true. Now, really, would any Marine steal or scrounge things from the Army?

Well, I will say one thing: Over the next few days, we seemed to eat better.

THE WELL

South Korea, 1951.

I think that I mentioned that scrounging was the right of every Marine.

It's not that we didn't receive supplies and equipment. It was just that all the other branches of the military seemed to have a better supply system than ours. In other words, somebody in Washington seemed to like them better.

Sometimes I think that we were considered the stepchildren of the military—always getting the hand-me-downs and secondhand items. Never invited to the ball unless there was trouble expected. And of course, since fairy godmothers didn't exist, we had to learn to make do with what we had . . . or with what they had.

Anyway, there seemed to be a lull in the war. At least, nothing major had happened in a couple of days.

We had set up a defensive perimeter in a farm and noticed that there were some chickens. Now, being aware of the fact that the South Korean peasant was very poor and figuring that he needed all his chickens, we immediately quashed any urges that we may have had in acquiring any of the chickens for our pot.

But where there are chickens, there are, of course, eggs. Now, if you were in any way familiar with the diet of a combat Marine in the field, you would know that the cooks used powdered eggs in all meals where the recipe called for eggs. But deep in the recesses of our minds, we remembered the taste of eggs cooked over-easy.

With this in mind, we approached the farmer and made the suggestion that he allow us to purchase some of his eggs or even to barter for some of his eggs.

Now, obviously this farmer was not aware of the fact that we were there to provide protection for him and his family, and to guarantee for him the right to choose to raise his chickens. I mean, after all, it was common practice for armies to appropriate any and all of the peasants' possessions.

Of course, being Marines, we would never take what was not offered.

We had a Marine with us who spoke Korean or at least seemed to be able to communicate with a combination of words and hand gestures. So with this Marine interpreting, we proceeded to try to enter into some sort of trade agreement.

But no matter how generous we were prepared to be, this farmer kept refusing our offers. Now, what kind of man turns down the munificent offers we were making?

After about two hours of fruitless negotiations, our Marine who was representing us grew a little

The Well 67

exasperated. Reaching into his pocket, he pulled out a bottle of water purification tablets.

He then proceeded to explain to the farmer that if he didn't start to negotiate in good faith, he would have no alternative other than to poison his well. He figured this was appropriate because that particular farmer was apparently filled with poison towards our generous offers.

The farmer chose to ignore this step in the negotiations. Now, having made the statement that if we weren't allowed to buy or trade for some of the farmer's eggs, we would be forced to poison his well.

The Marine opened the bottle of purification tablets and removed one.

Again asking the stubborn farmer to trade some of his eggs and still getting a negative shake of the head, the Marine reached his hand over the well and dropped the tablet into the well.

The shock on the farmer's face was indeed a sight to behold.

But again, the farmer refused to turn loose any of his eggs.

I mean, really, it wasn't like we were going to take his chickens. We were offering him such fantastic items in trade, and he would have more eggs tomorrow. I mean, this was one mean-spirited farmer.

Three more times, the Marine extended his hand over the well and released another tablet. Still, that mean-spirited farmer refused to part with any of his eggs.

Well, it was a sad thing to say, but our negotiator finally lost his temper. He opened the bottle and said, "The hell with you and your damned chickens and your damned eggs."

He then reached over the well and proceeded to pour the rest of the bottle of water purification tablets into the well.

The farmer crying and screaming and yelling went running off to find someone to complain to.

Deciding that discretion was the better part of valor, the Marines took off.

Now, I can't say if this story is true. But what I will say is that in the coming months, every time we suggested bartering for items of interest to us, the population seemed to be eager to comply. I do doubt that the incident of the eggs and the well had anything to do with it.

TORPEDO JUICE

The Marines, while known for their prowess in battle, have another talent. Any Marine worth his salt has been known to occasionally imbibe a wee bit of libation. Now, while Scotch and bourbon and whisky are usually the choices, Marines have been known to taste such things as vodka and gin and brandy. Hell, even an occasional drink of wine will suffice to bring a look of pleasure to one's face.

But, in the confines of the battlefield, these libations are not readily available. Never fear, Marines are known for their ability to rise to the occasion, even when it comes to booze.

The families that we had left behind in the States were made aware of the almost fanatical need the Marine had in being clean shaven. The Marines requested and the families responded to the repeated requests for Mennen after-shave lotion. I mean, really, how much danger could their Marine loved ones be in if they were constantly shaving?

The other thing that pleased the home folk was the fact that their Marines were obviously interested in maintaining a healthy body as many requested that they be sent cans of grapefruit juice.

Well, that is not exactly what the Marines had in mind.

There was not a whole lot of shaving going on. And grapefruit juice was an important ingredient in what was sometimes called "kick-a-poo joy juice" (from the Li'l Abner comic strip) or as the more seasoned Marines called it, "torpedo juice."

Marines had been known to turn their noses up to the packaged beverages that were available to them when they returned to the States, stating that after the good old T. J., the packaged stuff tasted like water.

Also, the T. J. became a wonderful trading item. The Korean civilians seemed to take a particular fondness in its consumption.

After a firefight or an artillery barrage, the first thing that was usually checked was the status of the good old Mennen after-shave.

One enterprising Marine, having procured a large supply of both the Mennen and grapefruit juice, opened a small stand similar to a child's lemonade stand. I think that he managed to send home almost $20,000. Unfortunately, after the officers found out about it, they ordered him to shut down his enterprise.

I do know that after Korea, the Marine had a profitable, if short, career as a manufacturer of white lightning. His concoction became a legend in the hills of Kentucky and Tennessee. To the chagrin of the

Torpedo Juice

revenuers, they were never able to find his still. Even in those days, there was no law against having an overabundance of after-shaving lotion and grapefruit juice.

I believe that after the Korean conflict, he was able to amass quite a fortune in ready cash and went on to purchase a large amount of Jack Daniels stock. After the war, this ex-Marine was known to throw some fantastic parties and barbecues. And the bar did a brisk business in his private concoction of torpedo juice.

BOSTON HILLBILLY

South Korea, 1951.

There was a sergeant in Easy Company, 2nd Battalion, 1st Marines. This sergeant was born and raised in Boston. We'll call him Mike (Mick) O'Bannian.

Now, I wouldn't want to say that Mick was prejudiced, but he did have a strong dislike for most things Southern. Now, as Mick was a very good sergeant, he managed to conceal this attitude from the men in his platoon. Never once did I ever hear him say anything that could be called anti-Southern, except for one thing: music.

Mick's taste in music was threefold:

1. Being a good Irish Catholic, he had a soft spot in his heart for religious renditions, Schubert's *Ave Marie* being one of them.

2. Being Irish, of course, he loved the Irish ballads such as *Mother McCree* and his rendition of *Danny Boy* sung in his beautiful Irish tenor. It would bring tears to your eyes.

3. And of course, classical music was very high on his agenda.

Now that I have given you a little insight into his character and upbringing, this brings us to the story I am about to relate.

Now as many people have suspected, a Marine was no stranger to a small drink or two. Hell, the most sought-after gift from home was Mennen after-shave. This mixed with a wee drop of grapefruit juice in a combat zone was like the ambrosia of the gods.

Now, I'm not one to cast aspersions on the Irish, being half-Irish myself, but Mick did have a taste for a wee drop or two.

One day we made a spectacular discovery in a burned-out building. We discovered a 55-gallon drum filled with wine. Now, I use the term "wine" very loosely. By my guess, I would say that we would have been extremely generous in thinking that more than one grape was used to ferment this marvelous brew.

Now, being good Marines and considering that we had discovered this wonderful gift on one of our scouting trips, we showed no hesitation in liberating it.

Well, Mick, being a generous soul as all we Irish are, decided to share our bounty with the other men of the company. And share he did. Now, not really knowing the acid content of this wonderful brew, we elected to empty the contents of the cookies in our C-rations

Now, Mick being Irish, insisted on tasting the purity of our plunder. After a good solid sip (as only we Irish

Boston Hillbilly

75

know how) Mick pronounced it fit to drink. And drink we did.

After two or three cans of this wonderful concoction, Mick, with his beautiful tenor voice, lifted it in song. Not one of the beautiful songs from the Mass. Not one of the lilting Irish ballads. Not one of the classical pieces that he usually sang.

No, Mick started to sing country. Knowing the dislike that Mick had always shown for the twangy tones of country or hillbilly music, I figured that Mick had now exceeded even his tremendous capacity for a taste of the bubbly.

One of the men had a guitar, and Mick borrowed it and started to sing a song I had never heard:

Sittin' on the bridge, drinkin' moonshine from my still,
tryin' not to think of my sister Jill.
Sittin' there in the pourin' rain,
listenin' to the sound of the lonesome train.
Wonderin' why my daddy had been put in jail,
knowin' where my sister was goin'
as she snuck down the trail.
Daddy's in the jail cell, holdin' onto bars.
Our dog Spot was killed chasin' after cars.
Life in this town is kinda hard.
No food in the house, except what we grow in the yard.
People say that we have no drive,
that we only do enough work to keep alive.
But you know that ain't necessarily so,
cuzz it ain't our fault that we be so po'.

Life in the hills ain't never been easy.
With no winders in the house, it gets kinda breezy.
Leavin' in the mornin' cuzz I joined the army of the USA,
gonna get three squares and a little pay.
Soon everything's gonna be just fine,
no more standin' in the welfare line.
They gonna help me finish the 6th grade.
They gonna give me shoes so I can march in the parade.
They like me cuzz I can shoot the eye outta blue bottle fly.
There ain't gonna be any enemy soldiers pass me by.

Anyway, I can't exactly remember the words but the voice was pure Ernie Tubbs.

Mick denied the whole thing, saying that he never in his whole life had he ever heard anything so ridiculous.

I won't say for sure whether this story is true, but I do remember that in the late '50s and early '60s, there was a country singer who just happened to have a little bit of an Irish brogue and such a beautiful tenor voice.

BRASS BALLS

There was a Marine from California, a reservist who had served in the Second World War. You know the one I'm talking about—"The War to End All Wars." Or was that the First World War? Well, it doesn't really make any difference as man in his infinite stupidity always figures that the current war is "the war to end all wars."

Anyway, this Marine (I'll call him Bill Bennett) was sitting aboard the Japanese LST QO73, cleaning his M-1 rifle and checking all his gear. I noticed that he had the holster to his 45-caliber automatic pistol positioned in such a manner as to cover his crotch.

I pointed out to him: "Bill, how can you sit there like that with that .45 digging into your stomach? That has to be the most uncomfortable feeling."

"Well," replied Bill, "before I left California, I promised my wife that I would do everything I could to protect the family jewels. She wanted to be sure that when I came back, my jewels would be large, bright, and totally intact. She said that while she reluctantly agreed to share me with the Marine Corps, she was damned if she was going to let me hock the family

78 *Other Heroic Events*

jewels. I promised her that I would do everything I could to safeguard them."

In the following days, Bill took a lot of ribbing. One Marine said that he had heard of the term "the brass balls of a monkey," but never thought that he would ever meet the monkey. Someone else suggested that it would have been much simpler if before Bill left California, he had gone to a sporting goods manufacturer and had an iron jock strap made. Someone else said that it would have been much better if his mother had knitted him a brass-ball warmer, instead of booties. Some even started calling him Achilles and asked him if, when he was a baby, hadn't his mom dipped his little balls in the river Styx?

Bill just smiled and took all the ribbing. Never once did he ever lose his temper or snap back at his tormentors.

Yongdong-po, September 19, 1951.

Our company was under heavy attack. Mortar shells were dropping all around us. We were huddled under a bridge, waiting for our forward elements to clear away the enemy. A mortar shell landed not six feet from Bill, shrapnel rising at a ninety-degree angle. A large chunk of shrapnel slammed into Bill with such force that he was thrown off his feet.

Someone yelled, "Corpsman! Man down!"

Looking over, we could see blood saturating his

Brass Balls 79

fatigues. The area around his crotch seemed covered with blood. A few minutes later, Bill was medi-vaced out and taken to a hospital ship.

Two weeks later, replacements arrived and with them was Bill. He looked fit as a fiddle. It seemed that the blood had come from a wound in his thigh. The only other injured part was his .45. The shrapnel had slammed into him with such force that the .45 had been destroyed. His balls were totally intact.

Bill earned the nickname "Mighty Balls." I'm quite sure that his wife was very pleased. The family jewels had been safeguarded.

Was this story fact or fiction? Well, the only one who knows for sure is me, and I don't intend to tell.

No, that may not be true.

For, if the story is real . . . then of course, Bill and his wife Kathy would also know.

And we must not forget the Bennett children. Wouldn't you like to meet Bill and Kathy's daughter? I think they named her Jewel.

Well, if it had been me, I know I would have named her Jewel.

K-9

While dug-in in the village of Koto-ri, a young Marine noticed a mongrel dog off in the bushes. The dog looked to be about four years old. It seemed to be all skin and bones.

Being from a farm community and having been taught that all animals were to be treated with kindness, the young Marine was able to entice the animal out from the bushes. He then proceeded to feed the dog from his K-rations. The dog ate like it hadn't seen food in months and from its appearance, it probably hadn't.

During the next eight or nine days, the dog never left the Marine's side. Where the Marine went, the dog followed.

Now normally, foxholes were occupied by at least two Marines. But heavy fighting had reduced the number of Marines available to defend the perimeter. So against all logic and safety, the young Marine found himself dug in alone.

The dog, never leaving the side of the Marine, of course also slept in the foxhole. The Marine, when not on 50% or 100% alert, slept when he could. And so did his companion, the dog.

One night, as the Marine slept, he was awakened by a soft growl of the dog. There in his foxhole was a Chinese soldier. It was a toss up as to who was more surprised, the Marine or the Chinese soldier.

The soldier seemed to recover faster and, in a lunging movement, started to attack the Marine. As it was about 40 degrees below zero, the Marine was zipped into his sleeping bag. It was like being in a straight jacket. He could not get to his .45 or his knife.

As the Chinese soldier moved toward the Marine with a knife in hand and started to stab at the Marine, the dog leapt at the Chinese soldier and clamped down on his throat.

The attack of the dog allowed the Marine to reach his holstered .45. As he slept with the .45 on full load, he was able to fire through the sleeping bag, killing the Chinese soldier.

In the struggle with the Chinese soldier, the dog received four or five slash wounds. The Marine yelled for the corpsman and, between them, they were able to stabilize the dog.

On the march out of Koto-ri, the dog accompanied the Marine. Like the Marine, it too was evacuated at Hungnam. On arriving in Masan, the young Marine located a children's orphanage and the dog was placed with them.

There is a strong probability that this story was true.

All I know is that a young Marine kept sending ten dollars a month to an orphanage in Korea and always asked how a dog was doing.

SUFFER THE LITTLE CHILDREN TO COME UNTO ME

The biggest tragedy in war is the creation of so many orphans. We, here in the States, are barely affected by that. Yes, there are many children who have lost a father and some who have lost a mother. But the loss of both parents is rare indeed.

In a place like Korea, this was all too common.

We don't have time to worry about the consequences of war, the houses and villages destroyed, the tragic killing of civilians. Nothing intentional, not by Marines.

But how can anyone remain untouched by the look of despair in the eyes of the little children, the innocents, the casualties of war?

It is heart-wrenching to see children three or four or five years old, looking in garbage dumps for something to ease their hunger. The tattered rags on their frail little bodies. The hopeless despair in their eyes.

Surely, someday there will be a reckoning.

There was a Marine air wing at K-18 that took it upon themselves to see what could be done. They gathered toys and clothes. They contributed money and did everything that they could to ease the pain and loneliness of these forgotten children.

One little girl came down with a very serious illness, one that the Korean doctors could not diagnose. As there was an Army doctor down in Pusan who, in civilian life, had specialized in pediatric medicine, one of the pilots flew the child down to Pusan to be treated by this doctor.

Massive doses of antibiotics were prescribed and, after about two weeks, the child was pronounced well.

The pilot was due for R&R in Japan and decided that he would take the little orphan to Japan with him. He contacted his wife, and she made arrangements to fly to Japan to see the child.

One of the hospital ships was due to sail from Korea to Japan to transfer a large number of wounded to the Army hospital in Tokyo. After offering a few tokens to one of the corpsman aboard the ship, arrangements were made to smuggle the child to Japan. When the ship arrived, the pilot and his wife were waiting at the dock.

After seeing the little girl, the pilot's wife decided that she had to adopt her. Because of the tremendous amount of abandoned and orphaned children in Korea, one of the Christian missions offered their assistance. Needless to say, the little girl left Japan thirty days later, accompanied by her new mother.

The amount of time and money, expended by the Marine air wing, managed to make life easier for

Suffer the Little Children to Come Unto Me 87

hundreds of children. Anyone who tells you that Marines have no heart or compassion has never met a Marine.

In 1972, Gwyn Booker received her medical degree in pediatric medicine. Her dad and mom were both there beaming with pride.

One couldn't help but notice the pride in their blue eyes for their daughter Gwyn. Many people commented on the fact that the name Gwyn seemed to be a little out of place for a young woman who was clearly Oriental.

The mother replied, "You know, sometimes genes can really do some strange things."

THE BIRTHDAY PRESENT

In any war, there are children who get caught up in its aftermath—children who lose their families or their village. These children are then on their own, forced to dig in garbage areas for enough food to sustain them. The story that I am about to tell you concerns one of these children.

After the Reservoir and the stay at Masan, the unit was ordered into battle. The fight to regain control of the territory south of the thirty-eighth parallel was both brutal and devastating. In the artillery and mortar attacks, many villages were destroyed. In most cases, this was the result of shells landing in the wrong area.

During one such battle, a small village was completely destroyed. Fortunately, there were not too many civilian casualties.

A few hours after the battle, we came across a young boy. He looked to be about twelve years old. He appeared to be hungry, dazed, and his clothing was in tatters. As many of the Marines had young brothers and young cousins in the States, it was not long before the child was taken under the wings of one of the platoons.

Some clothing was scrounged that came pretty close to fitting him. He was given a mess kit and became part of the platoon. Now, being a very proud people, the young Korean insisted that he earn his keep. So he would fetch water from the creek and gather wood for the campfires.

One of the Marines, a former schoolteacher, started to teach the boy English. In the course of the many conversations with the boy, it was learned that he had a birthday coming up in about six weeks. Wanting to do something special for the boy, one of the Marines wrote to his wife and asked her to see if she could find a Marine uniform that would fit the boy.

In the six weeks prior to the boy's birthday, we were under almost constant attack. No matter how many times we laid out a minefield, the enemy seemed to be able to penetrate it. We sent out scouting parties, looking for an enemy forward-observation post that had to be charting our mine positions. No matter how thoroughly we scouted the areas, we could find no sign of an enemy watcher. Yet, night after night, they managed to penetrate our positions.

The casualty rate among our men climbed. Our nerves were becoming frayed, and we were edgy as hell.

About a week before the boy's birthday, the package from the States arrived. Inside the box was a complete replica of a Marine green uniform. It was authentic in every detail. It even included a name tag sewn on the breast pocket with the name that we had given the boy—"KIM HO."

The Birthday Present 91

We set about preparing a birthday celebration the boy would never forget. All the Marines came up with a present for Kim, including a watch that one of the Marines had purchased from one of the Korean vendors. On the orders of the company commander, the baker was to bake a birthday cake for Kim. The wife, who had had the uniform made, had also sent birthday candles.

The day of Kim's birthday arrived and the party was a tremendous success. A good time was had by all. Kim oo-oohed and aa-aahed at each gift that he received. His eyes seemed to shine. I don't think that I had ever seen a more surprised and happy child in my life.

Then came the time to present the uniform to Kim. He was handed the box and, when he opened it, his eyes got as big as saucers. The thanks poured out of him like water from a dam. The interpreter then suggested that Kim try on the uniform.

Kim kept saying, "No, uniform too pretty. Want to save uniform to show family when they were found."

Excuse after excuse poured from his lips. Realizing that the boy was completely overwhelmed by the generous gifts and figuring that he felt he didn't deserve to be dressed like a Marine, we decided to put the uniform on him ourselves.

Two Marines grabbed him and started to strip him so as to put the uniform on him. And then . . . we knew why he didn't want to undress in front of us.

Strapped to his waist was a radio.

Kim, our young refugee, was actually Kim the Spy. He had been radioing the enemy each day the exact positions of our buried mines. Because of Kim, we had suffered over sixty Marines killed.

It took all the will power we had not to kill him.

Kim was turned over to the South Korean MPs.

In war, many things and many people are not what they seem to be. Looking back on the incident, I can see Kim for what he was—a North Korean patriot.

But at the time, all I saw was a rotten, ungrateful little bastard. I would imagine that in the hands of the South Koreans, he faced the same fate as Nathan Hale.

HALT!
WHO'S THERE?

A combat zone can be a terrifying place. Oh, hell, let's tell it like it is. It is definitely a terrifying place.

In the Marines, we usually post an outer perimeter watch. In this outer perimeter watch is something called a forward position. And when I say "a forward position," that is exactly what I mean.

We were dug in an area that was extremely prone to an attack. The unit was on 50% alert. That meant one man slept and one man watched. That was to prevent any chance penetration by enemy troops. Our casualties had been high, and we were expecting a major attack at any time.

As most attacks started in the dark of night, sound traps had been rigged to alert the watch to any activity in the fire zone. Also, a series of anti-personal mines had been laid.

One night, about 0500, the sentry at the forward position thought that he had heard some activity in his fire control zone. Waking his foxhole buddy and using the field radio, he alerted the sergeant-of-the-guard.

Leaning forward with both ears on alert, he strained to hear any movement. He went so far as to place his ear on the frozen ground to see if he could pick up any sound vibrations.

After about five minutes, he picked up a sign of movement. In a loud voice, following Marine Corps procedure, he yelled: "Halt! Who's there?"

There was utter silence from the area of the noise.

Once again, following procedure, he yelled: "Halt! Who's there?"

Again, there was no response. After a minute had passed, the double click sound of a 50-caliber machine gun was heard and then, in a very loud voice, the Marine was heard to shout: "YOU BETTER TELL ME WHO IS THERE OR I'M GOING TO FIND OUT WHO *WAS* THERE."

With that challenge, a flare burst in the air and there, before the eyes of the sentry, was the dog that the Major had found and adopted. The laughter that followed was loud and pointed.

The next day, the Marine took a lot of ribbing. It wasn't that we were being cruel. It was just so much relief that there had been no attack.

Unfortunately, the next night there was an attack and our friend, the Marine in his forward position, was one of the casualties.

I want to let everyone know that this was a true incident and that every time that I think about it, I thank God that our forward posts were so alert.

Sleep well, my friend.

THE POGGY BAIT CAPER

After bloody battles, many units are pulled off the lines and sent to the rear. This is to give the men a respite from hell and also to bring the units back up to strength.

After one particular bloody battle, our unit was pulled off the lines and sent back to a rest area. Now, while this was good news, as we needed the rest, we weren't exactly rolling in good things to cheer about.

On the third day of our rest, an Army unit pulled up and set up camp across the road from us. As luck would have it, a request came to our camp to borrow one of our corpsmen. It seemed that two of the Army units' medics had been wounded and they needed some medical help until medic replacements arrived. One of our corpsmen volunteered to assist the Army regiment.

The corpsman spent three days in the Army camp and then, after the medic replacements arrived, was told that he could return to his unit. While he was in their camp, he noticed that they had a good many supplies on hand that we did not. So, before returning to our camp, he borrowed a truck loaded with poggy

98

Other Heroic Events

bait (candy) and drove the truck and contents to our camp. He then proceeded to distribute the goodies to the Marines.

Some two hours later, two MPs arrived in our camp and took the corpsman into custody. He was to be brought up on a general court marshal.

Chesty, hearing of the arrest of the corpsman, sent a message to the Army colonel, requesting the release of the corpsman. He explained to the Army colonel that the Marines had been in a particular series of bloody battles and that the corpsman was just trying to bring some relief to the men. He also said that he would arrange a suitable punishment.

The Army colonel replied that he would not release the corpsman and that the corpsman would be charged with a general court marshal offense.

Again, Chesty sent a message, asking the Army colonel to reconsider. The Army colonel replied that he would be damned if he was going to release the man. After all, he was guilty of grand theft and, under the uniform code of military justice, he could be sentenced to twenty years in a federal penitentiary.

Chesty formed up the regiment and we marched across the road. On arriving there, he asked for the colonel to meet with him.

The colonel declined the invitation. Chesty then sent another message to the colonel, stating that if the colonel did not release his corpsman, then he would be forced to physically remove him from Army custody.

The Poggy Bait Caper

The colonel marched out of the camp at the head of his regiment and informed Chesty that he would be damned if he was going to be browbeaten by a bunch of candy-assed Marines.

Chesty replied that if the corpsman was not immediately released, he would take him. As the colonel started to reply that he wasn't about to release him, Chesty gave the order to fix bayonets.

As we smartly attached our bayonets to our rifles, the colonel, seeing that Chesty had every intention of storming the camp, ordered the corpsman released. As the corpsman arrived at the gate, Chesty took possession of the corpsman and in a very even voice, thanked the colonel. We then did an about-face and marched back to our camp.

He then sent a message asking the colonel if he wanted the poggy bait returned. The colonel in a gesture of good will decided that they really didn't need the candy back.

The above story was written to show the concern that Chesty had for his men. It has been said that anyone who ever served under him would have followed him to hell.

Watch out, Satan. We're on our way.

THE LAST OF THE KNIGHTS

You have heard the expression "being born in the wrong time." Well, I am about to tell you about a Marine officer who totally believed that he should have been born in the time of King Arthur.

He always regretted the fact that by the time he joined the Corps, the horse Marines were no more. He could picture himself astride a mighty charger, saber out, pointed towards the enemy, yelling "charge" as the thundering horse troop swept all aside.

Unfortunately, such a charge was not to exist. Even with his love for the old-time cavalry, he was still a highly skilled leader of Marine infantry.

We are going to give him the name of Croft—Captain Jim Croft.

Jim Croft had made the Inchon landing. He had been at the Reservoir. He had participated in the fight back to Hungnam and had been promoted to the rank of captain and awarded the Silver Star for bravery at the Reservoir. He was a company commander of Dog Company, 1st Marines.

After the Reservoir and the period of reforming the division, a series of battles took place in the months from January through April. These battles were as fierce and bloody as the Reservoir. It was like a tug-of-war. Take Hill 101 on Monday, pull back from Hill 101 on Tuesday, and retake Hill 101 on Wednesday.

There seemed to be no end to these battles and there was no rhyme or reason for them. But, as a good Marine officer, Jim Croft never questioned the orders. If they wanted to retake Hill 101, it was fine and dandy with him.

In early April, Jim Croft was ordered to take a series of hills. On the first three hills, no resistance was encountered. The fourth was a different kettle of fish. The fourth hill was heavily defended. Each time Dog Company got a foothold on the hill, the enemy counterattacked and Dog Company was pushed back. Causalities were heavy.

On the third day of this insane situation as the Marines once again started their climb back to the top, the enemy started a mortar barrage. It seemed that every time more than two or three Marines were close together, a mortar shell landed in their midst. Try as they could, Dog Company could not make any inroads in the defense of that stupid hill.

The morning of the fourth day, Jim Croft was nowhere to be seen. One of the platoon leaders, a young lieutenant, took charge of the company and started to attack up the hill one more time. The accuracy of the

The Last of the Knights

enemy mortars was unbelievable. The casualties incurred by Dog Company were brutal.

Just as the young lieutenant was about to order a pull back, the sound of a bugle was heard and charging out from the trees to the rear was the most amazing sight imaginable. There was Jim Croft, mounted on a white farm horse, knees tightly gripping the sides of the horse, with a bugle to his lips, blowing "charge" and his dress saber raised high.

Taking the bugle from his lips, he yelled: "FOLLOW ME, MEN! WE'RE GOING TO TAKE THIS DAMNED HILL TODAY, COME HELL OR HIGH WATER!" And with a mighty yell of "CHARGE," he proceeded to ride up the hill.

The stunned members of Dog Company gathered behind him and proceeded to climb that hill. Totally ignoring the mortars, the Marines started to gain access to the hill. Realizing that these mad fools must be stopped, the enemy mortar gunner started to drop his shells around Jim Croft and his horse.

Croft, screaming "COME ON, MARINES, DO YOU WANT TO LIVE FOREVER?" rode forward up the hill, yelling "COME ON, MEN, I'M GOING TO GET TO THE TOP OF THIS F—ING HILL OR DIE TRYING."

He kept up his relentless charge.

Well, Dog Company took the hill and Jim Croft did reach the top and he did get there before his men.

About twenty-five feet from the top, the enemy gunner dropped a mortar shell right on top of the captain and his horse.

And he was right, he and the horse got there. I can imagine the thrill that Jim Croft must have had as he looked down from Valhalla. That, it was clear, was the only appropriate place for this mighty warrior.

This story is one of my favorites. It fits the Marine Corps motto of *Semper Fi*. The Marines believe that in the heat of battle, God will look down on them and provide the means for victory.

I won't say for sure if this was a true story, but I can imagine the other warriors like Odin and Thor and even mischievous Loke, clustering around Captain Jim Croft and admiring his Navy Cross and saying, "Well done, sir, and welcome to the home of the eternal warrior."

FEAR IS IN THE EYE OF THE BEHOLDER

After I returned to the States, I was sent to the Naval hospital at Mare Island, California. About a year later, I happened to pass a newsstand in Philadelphia where I was continuing to recuperate.

Anyway, to get back to what I was saying, there, on the cover of a national magazine, was the picture of a Marine I had met in Korea. I bought the magazine, returned to my quarters, and proceeded to read the story.

I had not seen Paddy since he had been medi-vaced out in April of 1951. Paddy was quite a cutup. If there was some mischief to be done, Paddy was usually the one who instigated it.

Now, as Paddy was Irish, he had the innate ability that the Irish had to do two things well. One was drinking. Paddy had the Irish stomach, meaning that he seemed to be able to consume large quantities of whiskey with little or no outward effect. The second was that Paddy was a born clown. He claimed to have been a leprechaun in a previous life.

Normally when in the grip of either the booze or the tomfoolery, he was fun to be with. But every so

106 Other Heroic Events

often, Paddy was bitten by both Irish bugs at the same time.

In a village in China where Paddy was stationed, there was a government building. In front of the building was a flagpole and a mighty flagpole it was. It towered over most of the adjacent buildings. Now the fact that the Chinese flag flew higher than the Marine flag seemed to bother Paddy. So, as he was in the arms of quite a bit of the liquid Irish, Paddy set out to rectify this matter.

That night, Paddy left his quarters and proceeded over to the government building and proceeded to shinny up the flagpole.

When he reached the top, he attached the Marine flag to the top of the pole, cut the lanyard, and tied it off so that the flag could not be lowered. Then, he proceeded to climb down. Now, even in his besotted mind, Paddy knew that it would be an easy matter for one of the Chinese soldiers to climb the pole.

But Paddy had come prepared. From a backpack, Paddy removed a can of axle grease, which he proceeded to liberally apply to the pole as he inched his way down. With a pleased look on his angelic Irish face, Paddy and his bottle returned to his quarters

The next day, all hell broke loose.

The Chinese discovered the Marine flag and, realizing that the line had been cut, proceeded to try to climb the pole. But the more they tried, the more they failed.

It wasn't long before a very pissed-off official was on the phone to the Marine commander. The Marine commander denied that any of his men could have been involved, but did offer to assist in the removal of the flag.

After hanging up, the commander sent for Paddy.

"Paddy, I have no proof that you were the one to pull this dumb-assed trick, but you and I both know that you are guilty as hell. Now, you get your drunken Irish ass over to that building and get that flag down. I don't know how you are going to do it. I just know that you are."

Paddy realizing that he was probably in deep sh-t figured he had better do as the Colonel said and proceeded over to the building. After giving the matter some thought, a big Irish smile lit up his face.

Returning to the barracks, he proceeded to get two fire buckets filled with sand. Returning to the flagpole, he stripped down to his waist, tied the sand bucket around his shoulders, and proceeded to climb the pole. As he climbed, he spread the sand over the axle grease and advanced another foot.

It took him over an hour to reach the top. He gently removed the Marine flag, tucked it in to his belt, reached back into his backpack, removed a can of kerosene, and proceeded to apply it to the sand and axle grease, thus removing the mixture from the pole.

After he returned to the barracks, he cleaned up and reported to the Colonel. A reprimand was placed in his file and he was transferred back to the States.

Anyway, I was totally familiar with the story of the flag but what surprised me was the statement that Paddy had made in the magazine. And I quote from memory: "I think that I can honestly say that there was never a day in my life when I was scared."

In April of 1951, the Dog Company was under heavy mortar fire. The Marines of Dog were repeatedly thrown back in their attempt to take the hill they were trying to climb. The attrition rate was terrible. And then out of a clump of trees came this white farm horse. (See "The Last of the Knights.")

Astride the horse was, of course, Captain Jim Croft. Directly behind the captain and the horse was Paddy. Paddy was no coward. He was trying to climb the hill and reach their objective. When the mortar shell landed that sent Jim Croft and the horse to the top of the hill, Paddy had just grabbed the horse's tail for traction.

Part of the horse and part of Jim Croft was splattered all over Paddy. Paddy was thrown into a state of paralysis and shock. He was physically and mentally incapable of moving.

In plain words, Paddy was scared out of his mind.

The hill was quickly taken, and the helicopters were brought in to remove the wounded, Paddy among them.

You have to understand that Paddy was no coward. He had fought in many battles, not only in Korea but

Fear Is in the Eye of the Beholder 109

also in World War II. Paddy's good Irish genes had immediately thrown his mind into a defensive posture, blanking out all memory of what had taken place.

I guess Paddy could say that he had never known a day of fear because I doubt very much if Paddy remembered any part of what had happened. I truly hope that Paddy never did remember.

Here's to you, buddy. And may the good Irish whiskey turn to honey as it slides down your Irish throat.

WHAT PRICE BRAVERY

The lifeblood of a combat Marine can be said to literally be in the hands of the Navy corpsman attached to his unit. Thousands of Marines owe their lives to their corpsman.

This is the story of one of them. I am not going to use his last name. That's not to slight him or to try to keep his identity secret. It is because the fifty years that have passed have clouded this old mind from some things, last names being a case in point.

Charley was a corpsman. It doesn't mean that was his occupation. It literally means that Charley was a corpsman . . . in every sense of the word. Charley had fought in World War II. He had been a corpsman then and, after being recalled to active duty after the invasion of Korea, he was once again a corpsman.

This story is about Charley and I swear every word is true.

The fighting had been terrible. The casualties heavy.

Charley was attached to a unit that had been set up as an advanced perimeter defense. The unit came under heavy mortar and artillery fire. The Chinese

Communist soldiers were close enough to have been able to set up a deadly machine gun barrage. Casualties had exceeded fifty percent with no end in sight.

Fifty yards ahead of the unit was the forward perimeter position. There was no doubt that the Marines in the forward position had been wounded after letting battalion know the unit was ordered to pull back.

But there was one thing wrong with the order. Pulling back would be no problem. The problem was how to recover the men in the forward foxhole.

The company commander was willing to follow the orders but in true Marine Corps tradition, he wasn't prepared to abandon his men.

The captain gave the order to pull back and then proceeded to crawl forward towards the foxhole to try to bring his men out. He had crawled about thirty yards when he was hit in the spine and paralyzed.

He yelled, "CORPSMAN!"

Charley, hearing the cry, immediately started forward to attend to the wounded man. Running in a zigzag pattern, Charley was hit twice. He never slowed down.

On reaching the captain, Charley realized that he would not be able to assist in any way. Charley bent down, picked the captain up in a fireman's carry and proceeded to run back to the Marine lines. Dropping the captain, Charley then started back to finish the job and recover the men in the forward foxhole.

When he got to the Marines, he saw that two of them had been wounded very badly. So once again,

What Price Bravery 113

Charley grabbed one of the Marines and started back to the lines. Again he was hit—this time in the side.

On arriving back, he put the Marine down and went back for the other wounded Marine. This time, he received no more wounds. Picking up the last live Marine, he started back once again.

Before anyone could stop him, Charley stood up and again ran back this time to recover the dead Marine. God must have been watching over him because, this time, Charley drew no enemy fire.

Charley bent down picked up the dead Marine in his arms, stood up, and started a slow walk back to the Marine position. Not a shot was fired at him. It was as if the enemy soldiers were saluting Charley for his tremendous courage.

Arriving back, Charley gently put the body down and sat there and started to cry.

Thirty minutes later, the medical helicopters arrived to airlift the wounded out. When they tried to load Charley on the helicopter, he started to fight and scream that he couldn't leave.

"THERE ARE WOUNDED TO CARE FOR."

They finally had to sedate Charley and strap him in.

For gallantry above and beyond the call of duty, Charley was awarded the Navy Cross—the nation's second highest award. I believe that Charley should have received the Congressional Medal of Honor.

But it really wouldn't have made any difference to

Charley. You see, Charley never knew he had been awarded a medal. Charley was confined to the psychiatric ward of the Philadelphia Naval Hospital. A day doesn't go by that Charley doesn't relive that day over and over again.

Charley, if you are still alive, I can only wish freedom for you from your horrible nightmares.

Sleep in peace, Charley, wherever you are.

THEY SHALL COME FROM THE EAST

There was a young Marine who had been married to his high school sweetheart for almost four years. Alice had a job with an insurance company as a typist. In 1950, the military didn't provide much money and the kids needed all the income they could make.

Henry had been in the Corps for the entire four years and had just made corporal. When the Korean War broke out, Henry was stationed at Camp Lejeune in North Carolina. Marines from the 2nd Division, located at Camp Lejeune, received orders to prepare to be shipped to Camp Pendleton in California, the home of the 1st Marine Division. Henry was given a ten-day leave and then would be transported to California with the rest of his regiment.

Because the kids needed the money and Henry would be shipping out for the Far East in a matter of a couple of months, Alice decided that she would return to her parents' house in Dearborn, Michigan. Because she had been such a good employee, the insurance company agreed to allow her to transfer to an office in Detroit.

Henry wrote to Alice every day and called her at her mother's house once a week. On the day Henry was to ship out for Japan, he called Alice and spoke for almost fifteen minutes. He assured her that he would be fine and that he would be back as soon as possible.

Henry seemed to lead a charmed life. He made the Inchon landing and took part in the battle for Seoul. He never received so much as a scratch.

Henry was part of the first regiment under Chesty Puller and, in December, while leading a patrol, his unit was ambushed. Henry ordered two of the four-man patrol to dig in and sent the third Marine back to get help. In the initial attack, the radio had been damaged.

For two hours, Henry and his two men fought off the attackers. Both men were wounded and Henry ordered them to stay down. Taking a bag of grenades and a BAR (Browning automatic rifle), Henry started a one-man assault on the enemy. Henry did this to protect his two wounded men. With the BAR and the grenades, Henry managed to kill over fifteen enemy soldiers.

His luck held and he escaped without a scratch. Returning to his wounded men, Henry prepared to drag them out of the area, hoping to get back to the regiment before the Chinese soldiers renewed their assault.

Henry was in luck. A company of Marines arrived, and Henry and both of his men were escorted back to the regiment.

Henry, having been promoted in Seoul to Buck Sergeant, was now promoted to Staff Sergeant. Chesty

They Shall Come from the East

put him up for the Silver Star.

But Henry's luck ran out on the march back to Hungnam for the evacuation. On the march, Henry was frostbitten and later had three fingers amputated.

Henry decided that wasn't so bad. After all, he was right-handed and wouldn't really miss the three fingers from his left hand. Henry was sent back to the States and was discharged.

When he arrived back in Detroit, there was no one at the station to meet him. Figuring that it was kind of late for Alice to have come down to meet him, Henry took a taxi home to Dearborn.

When Henry walked into the house, he saw Alice sitting at the kitchen table. Alice turned and when she saw Henry, she started to cry.

Henry walked over and told her not to cry. He was fine and just glad to be home again with her. With that, Alice started crying even louder.

Henry said, "Everything's going to be fine, Alice. I told you in my letter that the wound wouldn't cause any problems and I was fine."

Sniffling Alice said, "Henry, I'm not crying for you. I'm crying for me. I'm pregnant."

With that Henry looked at her, bent down, picked up his bag and said, "I have to go East."

With that, he walked out the door and never came back.

Henry filed for divorce and, after it was granted, moved to Florida. Henry, being an avid fisherman, borrowed money on a GI loan, and bought a fishing boat. The years were good to Henry. His business prospered. He got married and had two kids. He put them through college and then left the business to the kids.

In 1981, Henry was eating in a restaurant in Fort Myers, Florida, when who should walk in but Alice.

After thirty years, Henry held no grudges so he called Alice over and asked if she would have dinner with him. Alice was more than pleased to see Henry.

Halfway through dinner, Alice asked, "Henry, will you answer a question for me please?"

"Sure," said Henry. "What do you want to know?"

"Henry, on the night you left, you said you had to go East. What did you mean?"

Henry started to laugh.

"I said I had to go East because the last time that there was a virgin birth, three wise men appeared from the East. I just figured I would hike out and meet them."

No, Henry and Alice never got back together. They were both happy with their lives and could see no reason to change them.

Way to go, Henry.

PART II
FROM THE BEACH
TO THE
RESERVOIR

Introduction and poem
written by Kal Kalnasy

Photographs courtesy of
Marine Corps University Research Archives

SEMPER FIDELES ALWAYS FAITHFUL

Semper Fideles: Always Faithful!

Since 1775, the United States Marine Corps have lived up to that slogan.

Through the centuries other elite forces risked life and limb to serve and protect. The tradition dates back to the Spartans, those legendary warriors who defeated the best-trained and best-equipped army in the known world. A band of 300 Spartans held off thousands of elite troops at the Battle of Marathon.

That feat went unequaled for 2,000 plus years, until Korea and the Marine Corps' defense of the Manchurian border; the towns of Udam-ni, Hagaru-ri, Koto-ri; and of course, the Chosin Reservoir. The Marine forces were outnumbered twenty-five to one, but still they were able to inflict heavy casualties.

Who were these troops defeated by the Marines? They were not some ragged, ill-equipped, untrained troops, but rather the best that China had to offer. The Chinese forces, arrayed against the 1st Marine Division, were troops that in many cases had been trained by Marines themselves.

China entered the Korean conflict with the full assumption that they would sweep away this undermanned Marine division. Expecting a rapid invasion and quick victory, they poured across the Yalu River. Using tactics first demonstrated by Ghengis Kahn, they attacked.

Whole American army divisions and Korean army units were pushed back by this relentless yellow horde. There seemed nothing in their way to accomplish a quick victory. And then, the amazing happened.

Like the Spartans of old, the 1st Marine Division not only held their positions, but also proceeded to push them back. This surprising feat accomplished by a few brigades and battalions of Marines allowed thousands of military personnel to withdraw from the field with honor.

The Marines, acting as rear guards in the spirit of Roland, blunted every charge made by the Chinese. For more than ten days, the Marines held the perimeter, inflicting massive casualties on Chinese troops. Even the well-trained Chinese troop concentrations were not enough to break through the defense. Wave after wave of Chinese shock troops hit the Marine lines and wave after wave of Chinese troops were thrown back.

Much has been said about the police action in Korea. Washington officials have classified this as a police action, not considering the Marines who allowed our forces to pull out in an orderly manner. This Marine action gave the United Nations troops the respite they needed.

Semper Fideles: Always Faithful 123

On returning from Korea, the Marines, instead of being honored as heroes, were literally shunted to secluded bases and hidden from public view. This was not done because they had not performed (as Marines have always performed), but was done to allow the public to forget that for the first time in American history combat troops were committed with no intention of winning.

Marines realize that when they are sent into combat, they will be subject to a high casualty rate. It is the very nature of a Marine to understand this. It was again to be seen in a later war in Vietnam. But every Marine knows that for the very survival of a democracy, there has to be men willing to sacrifice their lives for the protection of friend, family, and country.

Let us never again place the cream of our fighting men in harm's way without giving them the means and the backing to complete their mission.

This poem "From the Beach to the Reservoir" is dedicated to not only the Marines who fought and died in Korea and Vietnam, but to all Marines throughout history and to Marines of today and the future.

All I can say is "SEMPER FI."

—Kaneohe Bay, Hawaii
June 15, 2000

FROM THE BEACH TO THE RESERVOIR

Kal Kalnasy
Las Vegas, Nevada
February 22, 2000

Inchon, Korea 1950 There it is just ahead
I've been thinking of it
since they dragged me out of bed
Standing there by the ship's nets
On being alive in the morning
I'm taking no bets

Scrambling down the nets to the LCVP
Wondering if anyone will survive
especially me
The noise of the rockets and guns
pounding in my ears
Trying to stop shaking
trying to conceal my fears

The ramp is dropping
we're hitting the beach
Racing across the sand
looking for cover that I can reach
Terror in the afternoon
and even more terror at night
Courage, please don't leave me
especially if I have to fight
Digging your fox hole
at least five feet deep
Lord, if I don't dig it deeper
I'll never sleep
Then comes the word
"saddle up, we move out in five"
Heading for the Han River
when we get there, will we all be alive?

Waiting for the thirty-first army
they should be there at first light
I sure hope that when they get there
They are prepared to fight
They're marching out onto the field
like they're on public display
A mortar shell lands, they leave the field
I guess they're not to fight today
Our tanks are exposed
they're on the bridge with no place to go
Mortar shells are coming in
landing on the bridge and also below
Why did this happen, how could it be?
Look, there are dead Marines
one-two-three
Well, I'll be damned
look, I'm wounded in the ass
How? I know it's the only part of me
that was touching the grass
Finally we're breaking through
the Korean mortars are dead

Oh my God, don't look at my buddy
don't look at his head
Corpsman, Corpsman come quick
please save those you can
Not him, not my buddy, he's dead

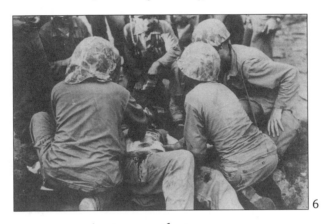

just save that man
Lord, none of this would've happened
if only the army had stayed
My buddy won't be home with his kids
he won't see them as they played
Here comes the chopper
I'm to be medi-vaced out
Someday I'll have to see his wife
and tell her what this was about
War can be so stupid and war can be so dumb
My god, what has happened?
Dear God, why am I so numb?
Here I am on a hospital ship
covered with a clean white sheet
Thinking, Lord, why them instead of me?
At this time, death would be so sweet

I don't think that we should cry
I think we'll just say
SEMPER FI

Out on patrol with twenty-one men
Don't know if we'll be back or when
Watch out, look to the right
I just caught a flicker of movement
in the moonlight
Hit the deck, hit the deck
as fast as you can
Come on, Marines
I don't want to lose another man
Come on, guys, keep your eyes peeled
what do you see?
There he is, at two o'clock
who's got the Springfield O-3?
Squeeze that round off
he's all yours
Breathe slowly, remember
we can't afford Maggie's drawers

On my motion, move forward
please keep low
That's it, keep your heads down
move low and slow
Intelligence reports there are gooks up ahead
Heads down, look sharp
I don't need any more dead
Up ahead, there's a house off to the right
You can just make it out in the morning light
You take the right flank
I'll move straight ahead
Look sharply, men
remember what intelligence said
Keep down, keep down
that's a rifle I see
I'm going to recon ahead
keep your eyes on me
There, off to the left in that clump of trees
Looks like a platoon of gooks grouped in threes
They're heading for that house
over by that ditch
I wonder if I should take out
that last son of a bitch
Lifting my arm
pumping one-two-three
Bringing my men up
grouping them next to me
Letting my men see what I had found
Telling them to be careful to hug the ground

Firing off a round from a three-point-five
Crawling forward to see if anyone is alive
There, at that window they're firing back
Jesus Christ, they got our radioman in the back
Open fire, men
blow those bastards to hell
"Corpsman, Corpsman"
I hear a Marine yell
The firing is so loud it sounds like the Fourth of July
Then, there's an explosion as fire lights up the sky
Checking my men to see who's dead or alive

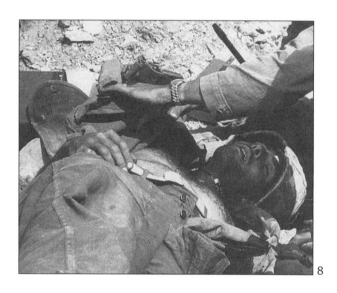

Eight men are wounded
My God, I've lost five
As much as I want to, I just can't cry
All I can say is
SEMPER FI

Driving through Korea like a runaway train
Not stopping for sun, cold, or rain
Sweeping opposition aside like so much trash
Eating our k-rations, sometimes ham, sometimes hash
North Koreans running as fast as can be
No fighting to speak of, no soldiers to see
Word comes down "there's trouble ahead"
Our convoys are being ambushed or so they've said
Marines are stretched out to the Manchurian border
"Into the trucks, keep them covered" is the order

We'll try to surprise them
it's the supply convoys they attack
If they ambush us
we'll be prepared to strike back
The roads in this part of Korea are rough and narrow

You would swear
they're not wide enough for a wheelbarrow
At the head of the column is a Patton tank
We huddle in our trucks, no matter our rank
The road is shaped with twists and curls
We sit in our trucks, napping and thinking of girls
The lead tank goes around the bend
and disappears from sight
Suddenly there's an explosion
loud enough to give you a fright
Then the sound of machine guns
as they open fire on you
No one killed in our truck
but they've wounded a few
We leap from the truck as fast as can be
Searching the hillside, yelling "what do you see"
There, by that tree
I see two-three-or-four
Killing them with a light machine gun
looking for more
We've smashed the attack, we've made them pay
My men and I are safe for another day
The road must be cleared
so we can get on our way
We must supply our forward Marines
before the end of the day
While the supply trucks continue
towards the Manchurian border

We dig in at a place called Koto-ri
and bring the camp to order
The engineers build an airstrip
cut out of the field
Orders come down from Colonel Chesty Puller
"We will not yield"
Rumors start flying
that Chinese troops have been seen quite near
What happened to the promise
we'd be home by the end of the year?
We do what Marines do and do so well
dig foxholes and prepare
God, don't let them attack
please tell me they wouldn't dare
I'm going to grab some sleep or at least try
What more can I say except
SEMPER FI

The sounds of bugles
break the stillness of the midnight air
Those eerie sounds seeming to come from everywhere
The ground vibrating from the rumble
of horses hoofs in the night
I crawl out of my sleeping bag
not knowing if I should run or fight
Word comes from Yudam-ni
"the Chinese have entered the war"
They've crossed over from Manchuria

with three divisions or more
They're being cut down like stalks of corn
they're piled six and seven high
We don't know if they can be stopped
but we've got to try
We're out of ammo
"fix bayonets" comes the cry
As we charge, they retreat
I guess they don't want to die
"Pull back, dig in"
are the orders that we receive
Here they come again
like water through a sieve
Our perimeter is collapsing
we're being overrun
Get our wounded and our dead
keep firing that machine gun
Then comes the most beautiful sight
the corsairs are here
Guns and bombs and napalm to the Chinese
bring nothing but fear
Under cover of the massive air attack
We are able to regroup as we pull back
This is not a retreat
that is something Marines never do
We are just attacking from a different view
We fight our way back to Hagaru-ri
bringing our wounded and dead

Winter is here, the temperature's dropped
just one more thing to dread
Writing letters home sayin' everything's fine,
everything's dandy
Sipping on a hot cup of joe
but keeping your rifle handy
Sending out scouting parties at dawn
trying to take a prisoner or two
Coming back after six hours in the hills
with fingers turning blue

Trying to keep the lines open
to prevent the Chinese troops
From overrunning our positions
destroying their attaching groups
Three thousand men
bottled up at the Chosin Reservoir
They need a safe place to regroup
before the Chinese kill any more
Chinese attacking again and again
trying to overrun our position
Trying to kill as many as we can
sending them to perdition
Bulldozers digging a hole in the frozen ground
to bury our dead
Enemy fire so heavy
our wounds and blood are running red
Evacuating our wounded by cargo plane
with tanks leading the way
Firing at everything straight ahead
making the Chinese troops pay
Maintaining our defensive positions
is more valuable than gold

No matter how many Chinese attack
we're totally committed to hold
Counting our wounded and counting our dead
makes one want to cry
Yet all I can do and all I can say is
SEMPER FI

Again and again the Chinese ninth army group
charges in another attack
Again and again the first, the fifth,
and the seventh Marines throw them back
Casualties are heavy we're dying one by one
yet nobody runs
We dig in deeper, close our ranks
and teach them the law of the guns
Wave after wave of screaming Chinese

14

throw themselves at our lines
they're killed by our Marines with rifles, mortars,
and hidden land mines
Still they keep coming like pigs to the slaughter
we wonder when it will stop
We pile them up two and three high
and still they come over the top
We throw ourselves to the ground
so our machine guns can do their work
Then up on our feet with bayonets fixed
we meet them like we've gone berserk
Cutting and slashing, lunging and parrying
we meet them face to face
We scream, we holler, we lunge
we kill of reason, there is no trace
We push them back, but at what cost

more Marines are lying dead
You know in your mind that soon you'll be killed
but still you move ahead
You hear the sounds of Chinese bugles
calling their units back
On the cold ground with a cigarette and cup of joe
waiting for the next attack

Marine fighters blanketing the sky
dropping napalm all around
You roll up in a blanket, grab some sleep
your body hugging the ground
Then comes the word "the rest of our Marines
from Hagaru-ri are coming" in a wave
Here they are, carrying their wounded and dead
I've never seen anything so brave
We tighten our lines and close our ranks
so we can give them a little rest
For in all the history of the Marine Corps
these men are by far the best
We know that for every Marine lost
The Chinese have lost twenty-five
We're bound and determined that whatever it takes
we will keep them alive
For ten days and ten nights
we hold our lines as casualties continue to mount

We have killed so many attackers
that after a few days, we no longer count
Then word comes down
"break camp, prepare to move out at first light"
We start the long trek back to the sea
and with every step taken, we fight
On the hills to our right and the snow to our left
the Chinese are everywhere
The wind is so cold the temperature drops
we fire our weapons with care
We open our mouths, take deep breaths
it feels like our lungs will freeze
One of the greatest fears that we have
is that we'll have to sneeze
As dusk settles in, we are ordered to camp
to dig our foxholes deep
We finish our jobs, then pull down our tents
and march again with no sleep

Casualties mount, frostbite sets in
many of us find it difficult to walk
We keep plodding on, fighting every inch of the way
too tired even to talk

Finally we arrive at the port of Hungnam
and see the harbor filled with ships
We fight our way to the boats
crawl aboard with a thank you on our lips
During the march, fighting every inch of the way
I thought I would die
Now on the evacuation ship
all I can say is

SEMPER FI

Photographs

Courtesy Marine Corps University Research Archives

1 LSU's Rendezvous near Command Ship *USS Mt. McKinley*.

2 Landing Craft Rendezvous Prior to H-Hour.
(*photos 2 and 4 have same caption*)

3 Control Vessels Prepare for the Landing on Wolmi.

4 Landing Craft Rendezvous Prior to H-Hour.
(*photos 2 and 4 have same caption*)

5 Men of 1st Marines Overlook Han River, near Yong-Dong-Po.

6 First Aid Is Administered to Marine near Sosa-Ri.

7 1st Marines at Yongdung-po, 9/19/50 Marine Rescued Under Heavy Fire.

8 A dying Marine, on the road to Seoul. c 9/50.

9 Marines break camp as a heavy snow storm sweeps Koto-ri, 8 Dec 50.

10 First Marine Division takes to the road on withdrawal from Koto-ri. Hdqtrs. No. A-5358, Defense Dept. photo (Marine Corps), Sgt. F. C. Kerr.

11 A combat patrol moves through snow fields in valley near Koto-ri, 8 Dec 50.

12 Crewman of an 81mm mortar, fire hasty mission from roadside position south of Koto-ri. 8 Dec 50.

13 It was necessary to bury the dead at Koto-ri. Every vehicle would be needed to carry vital equipment and wounded. 8 Dec 50.
(photos 13 and 15 have same caption)

14 Marine Rear Guard Protects Withdrawal From Yudam-ni.

15 It was necessary to bury the dead at Koto-ri. Every vehicle would be needed to carry vital equipment and wounded. 8 Dec 50.
(photos 13 and 15 have same caption)

16 U.S. Marines rest in the snow during move south from Koto-ri, December 8, 1950. Hdqtrs. No. A-5359, Defense Dept. photo (Marine Corps).

17 Side by side, bodies of British Royal Marines, American Soldiers, South Koreans, and our own Marines are buried at Koto-ri. 8 Dec 50.
(photos 17 and 19 have same caption)

18 Nothing stops the Marines as they march south from Koto-ri, fighting their way through Chinese Communist hordes in sub-zero weather of mountains. Despite their ordeal, these men hold their heads high. Picture taken 9 Dec 50. Hdqtrs. No. A-5372, Defense Dept. photo (Marine Corps).

19 Side by side, bodies of British Royal Marines, American Soldiers, South Koreans, and our own Marines are buried at Koto-ri. 8 Dec 50.
(photos 17 and 19 have same caption)

20 Troops of RCT 7 move into attack on road to Chinhung-ni, 8 Dec 50.